Teaching

for

Thinking

Mathematics

John Prince
Stephanie Burgoyne

GRAPHICS

Alexander Prince

Initial code for some diagrams and designs were obtained from posts at
    `http://tex.stackexchange.com,`
and TeXexample.net
    `http://www.texample.net/tikz/examples.`

CONTENTS

Contents

PREFACE

This book explores and examines mathematics and its role in elementary education. Strategies are given for teaching mathematical principles including problem solving and its integration with other subject areas.

Math is not 'just one problem after another', but most questions can be answered using several different methods. Some methods of thinking are more inventive and elegant than others, but all accurate methods will agree on both a reasonable initial estimate and the final answer.

Chapter 1

PROBLEM SOLVING

Throughout this book, you will be presented with numerous math concepts and methods of illustrating them. The corresponding problems and questions will include different methods of solving but regardless of the method *the final answer must be the same*. Especially if you are working alone, check your answer using an alternate method.

George Polya (1887-1985) was born in Hungary and held various university positions in his career both in Europe and in the United States. He made significant contributions as a mathematics teacher and researcher. His book *How to Solve It*, published in 17 different languages and released with significant sales.

In his book[1] Polya describes a four step problem solving process, as outlined in the following.

- Understand the problem

- Select a problem solving strategy

- Follow through on the strategy (strategies) chosen

- Look back on the solution, check over the work

Understanding the problem may involve highlighting the keywords, making a list of given information, developing a diagram or rewording the question. A problem may have extra information or missing information so the student needs to gather all relevant information in this step. Students may encounter words like sum, difference, product, quotient or expressions like "how much more", "how many in total", "how many groups". The understanding the problem stage is a critical step in beginning the

---

[1]https://notendur.hi.is/hei2/teaching/Polya_HowToSolveIt.pdf

problem solving process.

There are numerous problem solving strategies available and frequently there is more than one possible strategy for a given problem. Guessing and checking is a favourite strategy where students try various numbers and use higher or lower estimates to arrive at a solution. Diagrams, pictures and models are beneficial especially for geometry and measurement problems. Making a list or a table can help to reveal a pattern which in turn can be expressed as an equation. Sometimes a readymade formula is available for answering a word problem, such as in the case of perimeter, area or volume questions. Thinking of a number or missing number problems often use a working backwards strategy while solving a simpler problem is useful for a question with large or difficult numbers.

Once a strategy has been selected, then it is time to carry out the problem solving plan and solve the question. This step often requires time, patience and creativity and it may be conducted independently or in a group setting.

Looking back is an important step for students and teachers to check, share, display and discuss various solutions. Through sharing, students can discover other strategies, perhaps even more efficient strategies. Students are encouraged to make observations and generalizations of the solutions. Could they have used a simpler or more effective method? How can they apply this strategy to other problems? Is there a general statement or conclusion to help with future problem solving?

1.2   Examples of Solving Strategies

Example 1.2.1. *A gardener has* 20 *m of fencing for a rectangular garden. What whole number dimensions will produce the maximum area?*

▶ *Solution.*

STEP 1

Just as a student searches for keywords in the first step of problem solving so the teacher also selects the words to motivate certain mathematical operations and strategies.

In this example, the following keywords are important in communicating the word problem: fencing, rectangle, 20 m, whole number, dimensions, maximum and area. The word fencing invites the student to think of perimeter as the sum of the outside dimensions. The word rectangular tells the reader that we have four sides to fence with opposite sides equal and also includes the possibility of a square. Whole number rules out the use of decimals or fractions in the dimensions. The question of maximum area requires the problem solver to explore different areas to discover the largest possible result.

STEP 2 AND STEP 3

A teacher can envision various strategies that students might use to solve a word problem. Students can work individually or collaboratively to combine several strategies. The above example provides opportunity for diagrams, formulas, tables, models as well as guess and check.

Graph paper is helpful to make diagrams of various rectangles where the perimeter is 20 m and square tiles are also useful to build models of such rectangles. The possibilities can be summarized in a table where the area formula can help to determine through guess and check which area is the largest.

Length (m)	Width (m)	Calculation (m^2)	Area (m^2)
1	9	1×9	9
2	8	2×8	16
3	7	3×7	21
4	6	4×6	24
5	5	5×5	25
6	4	6×4	24
7	3	7×3	21
8	2	8×2	16
9	1	9×1	9

The table illustrates systematic guessing and checking from which a pattern emerges. As the length and width become closer together, the area of the rectangle increases. The maximum area occurs when we have a specialized rectangle, the square.

STEP 4

This step is a powerful step for both teacher and student as students share problem solving strategies. There are numerous questions to ask:

- What strategies worked most efficiently?

- What can be learned from the problem solving of peers?

- How can these results be applied to a future problem?

- What generalizations can be made from this problem?

The above problem makes connections between geometry and number sense can evolve through different grade levels, from the concrete models and guessing and checking of elementary grades to an optimization problem of a quadratic function for high school. ◀

Example 1.2.2.

Janet is saving for a bicycle which has a total cost of $180. She has saved $72 so far and she can save $12 each week from her allowance. In how many more weeks will she have enough savings to buy the bicycle?

▶ *Solution.*

STEP 1

The information that students might highlight include costs $180, saved $72, earns $12 each week, how many more weeks. This is a multi-step word problem which might require several readings to decide on a plan.

STEPS 2 AND 3

A teacher might expect guessing and checking, making a table or using algebra as potential strategies that students could explore. A table could provide a systematic method of the weekly total savings.

Week #	Savings ($)
Start	72
1	84
2	96
3	108
⋮	⋮
7	156
8	168
9	180
10	180

If the *number of weeks required to save for the bicycle* is represented by n, the situation is represented by $72 + 12n = 180$. The equation can be solved by guessing and checking or by algebraic reasoning.

ALGEBRAICALLY

$$72 + 12n = 180$$
$$72 + 12n - 72 = 180 - 72$$
$$12n = 108$$
$$\frac{12n}{12} = \frac{108}{12}$$
$$n = 9$$

STEP 4

As students look back on their solutions, they might ask:

- Is there a more efficient method to solve this problem?

- What can be learned from the solutions of other students?

- Is this problem similar to a previous problem?

- How would the answer change if Janet needed $185?

Teachers can vary this problem starting from a simple guessing and checking problem with smaller numbers to a linear relations problem with decimal numbers.

Example 1.2.3. *The probability that Kyle scores at least one goal during a hockey game is $\frac{5}{6}$. Design an experiment to simulate Kyle's scoring success in the next 15 games. Carry out the experiment to determine the number of games (in the next 15 games) in in which Kyle scores.*

STEP 1

This is an open-ended problem where answers may vary and where students may use their own creativity of design. The key ideas that the teacher has presented in the question and that the students would be expected to withdraw from the question are: probability, $\frac{5}{6}$, experiment, 15 games, scores. The students might have questions about this open-ended problem regarding the type of design, the materials for design, the preparation for the experiment. These questions can be addressed as the student moves from step 1 into step 2 (plan)

Steps 2 and 3

The problem invites students to use the problem solving strategy of making a model: a spinner with 6 regions (5 of which represent score), a die (where numbers 1 to 5 represent score), 6 pieces of paper in a hat (5 of which labelled score), 6 cubes (5 of the same colour to represent score and the other of a different colour). This problem encourages collaboration in setting up the model and in carrying out the simulation. During step 3 (actual experiment), one student can repeat the measure while the other student records the results in the form of a tally/frequency table.

Step 4

As students compare their results for the experiment, they can discover that although a theoretical probability can be calculated for the experiments, the actual experimental probability can vary dramatically. ◀

Exercises

Exercise 1.1. Use the four step problem solving process to solve the following problems:

a) Pamela has received marks of 68, 84, 72 and 79 on her first four quizzes. What mark does she need on her fifth quiz to obtain an average of 75?

b) I am thinking of a number. When I square the number, double that answer and subtract 4, the final answer is 68.

c) Given 2, 9, 28, 65, 126, ..., find the next term in the number sequence. Explain the pattern in words.

d) Determine the dimensions of a rectangle formed by nine squares with individual side lengths of 1, 1, 3, 4, 4, 5, 5, 6, 6 units.

e) Determine the dimensions of a rectangle formed by nine squares with individual side lengths of 1, 4, 7, 8, 9, 10, 14, 15, 18 units.

Chapter 2   SET THEORY

2.1   Sets of numbers

A set is simply a collection of objects or people. We have sets of books in our libraries, sets of CD's in our music collections, sets of people in our classrooms and families.

In math, we are interested in sets of numbers, sets of geometric figures and sets of equations. We can express sets in mathematics in different ways.

a) Using words: "The set of whole numbers that are divisible by 3 and that are less than 20"

b) Using lists of objects inside set brackets: $A = \{0, 3, 6, 9, 12, 15, 18\}$ With words, it is important to use specific language. In the listing format, we use commas to separate set elements. If the set is finite, we can list the elements but if the set is infinite, we need to list enough elements to establish a pattern, then we use an ellipsis, as in $B = \{0, 3, 6, 9, 12, \ldots\}$.

c) A third method of communicating about sets is set builder notation. In this notation, we use algebra and symbols to communicate the elements of set.

$$A = \{x \mid x = 3n, 0 \leq n \leq 6, n \in \mathbb{W}\}$$

The vertical line means 'such that', the Greek symbol $\in$ means 'belongs to' or 'is a member of', and the symbol W represents 'the set of whole numbers'. The notation reads 'A is the set of numbers x such that x equals 3 times a number n, where n is between 0 and 6 inclusive, and n is a whole number'. To find the elements of set A, we can substitute the given values of n into the equation $x = 3n$ using a table of values.

n	x
0	$3\,(0) = 0$
1	$3\,(1) = 3$
2	$3\,(2) = 6$
3	$3\,(3) = 9$
4	$3\,(4) = 12$
5	$3\,(5) = 15$
6	$3\,(6) = 18$

So $A = \{0, 3, 6, 9, 12, 15, 18\}$, is the same finite set as we communicated with words and listing in the previous examples.

How would this set change if we changed the equation to $x = 4n$? $x = 5n$? Our set would be multiples of 4 or 5 instead of multiples of 3.

How would set A be different if we changed the possible values of n to $1 \leq n \leq 4$? Or $n \geq 5$? We would substitute different values of n into our equation to obtain $\{3, 6, 9, 12, \ldots\}$ or $\{15, 18, 21, \ldots\}$.

We can also change the number system used in set builder notation by replacing whole numbers with another set such as natural numbers, or integers. The following are important sets of numbers which form the basis for mathematics. These are listed in the order in which we learn these systems in school.

Number Set	Set Notation
Natural	$\mathbb{N} := \{1, 2, 3, \ldots\}$
Whole	$\mathbb{W} := \{0, 1, 2, , \ldots\}$ (or $\mathbb{N}_0$)
Integer	$\mathbb{Z} := \{\ldots -3, -2, -1, 0, 1, 2, 3, \ldots\}$
Rational	$\mathbb{Q} := \{\frac{a}{b} \mid a, b \in \mathbb{Z}, b \neq 0\}$
Irrational	$\mathbb{Q}' := \{\text{non-terminating with no constant set of repeating digits}\}$
Reals	$\mathbb{R} := \mathbb{Q} \cup \mathbb{Q}'$

The rational numbers include any number that can be written as a fraction. These numbers include repeating decimals, terminating decimals, proper and improper fractions, integers and whole numbers.

The irrational numbers include $\pi, e, \sqrt{2}$, and any other decimals that do not repeat any set of digits. For example, $10.25\,225\,2225\ldots \in \mathbb{Q}'$ and cannot be written as a fraction.

Real numbers include both rational and irrational number sets: $\mathbb{R} = \mathbb{Q} \cup \mathbb{Q}'$

2.2   Euler and Venn diagrams

Sets and their relationships can be illustrated by a diagram, often using an Euler or Venn diagram. Circles or ellipses are often used but any shape is acceptable. Venn diagrams are Euler diagrams but Venn diagrams require that all possible options be illustrated. This is not a requirement of Euler diagrams.

For information on Euler, see

`http://scienceworld.wolfram.com/biography/Euler.html`

For information on Venn, see

`https://www.teachervision.com/mathematicians/biography/6132.html`

The universal set U is defined as the set of numbers or objects involved in a particular question and usually is constructed as a rectangle containing the other shapes. Generally, these diagrams have two to four[1] circles or ellipses. When there are more than four sets, the diagram organization become cumbersome.

A Venn diagram requires $2^{\{\text{number of sets}\}}$ distinct regions. If any region has no elements, the corresponding region will be shaded black.

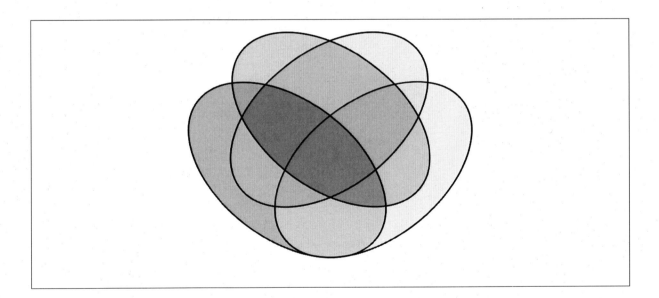

Figure 2.2.1: Venn diagram with four sets, $2^4 = 16$ regions.

The classic type of Venn diagram is the one that we can use as a graphic organizer for compare and contrast language assignments. This consists of two overlapping circles inside of a rectangle.

---

[1]http://eagereyes.org/techniques/venn-diagrams

Example 2.2.1. *Let* $A = \{1, 2, 3, 6, 12\}$, $B = \{1, 2, 5, 10\}$ *and* $U = \{1, 2, 3, 4, 5, 6, 7, 8, 9, 10, 11, 12\}$ *where U is defined as the universal set for this example i.e. no other numbers will be considered. Illustrate the connections between the sets using a Venn diagram.*

▶ *Solution.*

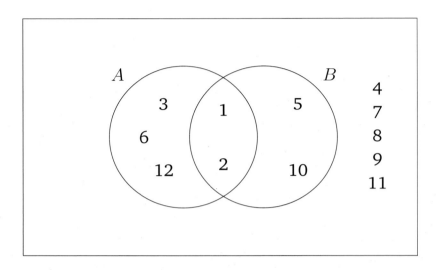

There are four regions to a Venn diagram with two sets, $2^2 = 4$: the numbers in only in A, the numbers only in B, the numbers in both A and B, and the numbers in neither A nor B. ◀

Definition 1 (Mutually Exclusive). *If two sets have no elements in common, they are said to be mutually exclusive. Their relationship can be best illustrated by an Euler diagram with two disjoint (separate) circles.*

Example 2.2.2. *Illustrate the sets of even and odd numbers using the counting numbers from 1 to 10 inclusive.*

▶ *Solution.* [Euler diagram]

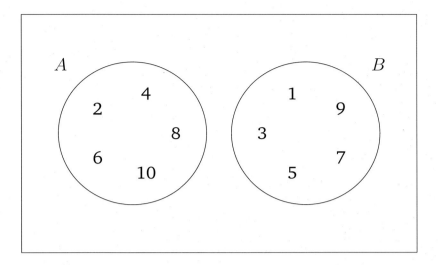

There is an infinite list of other counting numbers that exist. Those elements would be placed outside of the two circles.

This situation of disjoint sets could also occur when we carry out a sorting activity involving only two shapes, such as triangles and quadrilaterals.   ◄

Example 2.2.3. *A third possible diagram occurs when one circle is contained within the other circle. Given the universal set* $U := \{1, 2, \ldots, 10\}$, $A := \{2, 4, 6, 8, 10\}$, *and* $B := \{4, 8\}$, *illustrate the relationships between the sets.*

► *Solution.* [Euler diagram]

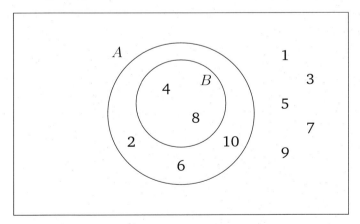

In this case, we say that elements of the inside circle are a subset of the elements of the outside circle (symbolized as $B \subset A$) In the first diagram, $B = \{4, 8\}$ is a subset of $A = \{2, 4, 6, 8, 10\}$ since every element of B is also an element of A.   ◄

Example 2.2.4. *Organize the set of quadrilaterals using a Venn or Euler diagram.*

▶ *Solution.* The set of squares is a subset of the set of rectangles because every square is a rectangle (but the converse is not true). Squares are also a subset of the set of rhombuses (but the converse is not true). Also, the set of rectangles is a subset of the set of parallelograms because every rectangle is a parallelogram.

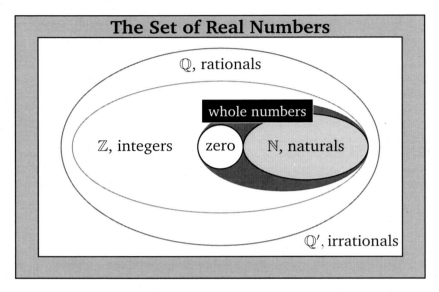

Figure 2.2.2: Illustration of relationships of the standard number sets.

◀

2.3   Unions, Intersections, Complements

The union of two sets, symbolized as $A \cup B$, includes all the elements that are in A, or B, or in both sets. The intersection of two sets, symbolized as $A \cap B$, includes all the elements that are in A and B. It is the overlap of the two circles A and B in the Venn diagram. For disjoint sets, the intersection is an empty set, symbolized as $\{\}$ or $\varnothing$.

The complement A^c of a set A is the set of elements in the universal set U that are not in A. The following example illustrates these set operations and the order of operations for sets.

Example 2.3.1. *Given*

$$
\begin{aligned}
U &:= \{1, 2, 3, 4, 5, 6, 7, 8, 9, 10\} \\
A &:= \{1, 2, 3, \quad\ \ 6 \qquad\quad\ \} \\
B &:= \{1, 2, \quad 4, \qquad 8 \quad\ \ \}
\end{aligned}
$$

a) Construct a Venn diagram of the three sets.

b) *List the elements of $A \cup B$*

c) *List the elements of $A \cap B$*

d) *List the elements of $A^c \cup B^c$*

e) *List the elements of $(A \cap B)^c$*

▶ *Solution.*

a) Venn diagram

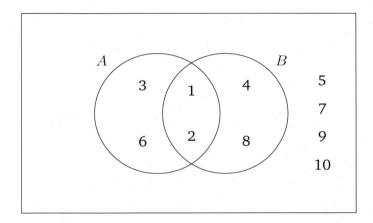

b) $A \cup B = \{1, 2, 3, 4, 6, 8\}$ Elements in A or B or both.

c) $A \cap B = \{1, 2\}$ Elements that are common to A and B

d) $A^c \cup B^c = \{4, 5, 7, 8, 9, 10\} \cup \{3, 5, 6, 7, 9, 10\} = \{3, 4, 5, 6, 7, 8, 9, 10\}$ Find the complement of each set first, then select the elements in A^c, B^c, or both.

e) $(A \cap B)^c = \{1, 2\}^c = \{3, 4, 5, 6, 7, 8, 9, 10\}$ Determine the intersection inside the brackets, and then determine its complement.

◀

Notice that operations in brackets need to be completed first, then any complements, then remaining unions and intersections from left to right. Also, it is interesting to observe that the answers for parts d) and e) are the same. It is true in general that $A^c \cup B^c = (A \cap B)^c$. Similarly, it can be shown that $A^c \cap B^c = (A \cup B)^c$.

2.4   Subset investigation

As we observed in our third type of diagram (circle within circle), B is a subset of A if all the elements of B are also elements of A. The set B is contained within the set A. There is a pattern for the number of subsets that can be made from a given set.

Consider the set $A = \{1\}$ which has only one element, the number 1. This set has only 2 subsets, namely $\{1\}$ and the empty set $\{\} = \varnothing$. The empty set is a subset of every set as we always have the option of not choosing any elements when forming any subset.

Next, consider a set $B = \{1,2\}$ with 2 elements. This set has 4 possible subsets, $\{1\},\{2\},\{1,2\}$, or $\{\} = \varnothing$. We can choose one element at a time, two at a time, or neither element.

As we continue this investigation, let's look at set $C = \{1,2,3\}$ and set $D = \{1,2,3,4\}$. For set C, we have 8 subsets by taking all possible combinations of the elements of C.

Number of Elements	Subsets	Number of Subsets
0	$\varnothing$	1
1	$\{1\},\{2\},\{3\}$	3
2	$\{1,2\},\{1,3\},\{2,3\}$	3
3	$\{1,2,3\}$	1
		8

What is our prediction for the number of subsets of set D? The pattern so far is 2, 4, 8 and if this continues, we would expect 16 subsets for D. Let's check by listing all possibilities.

Number of Elements	Subsets	Number of Subsets
0	$\varnothing$	1
1	$\{1\},\{2\},\{3\},\{4\}$	4
2	$\{1,2\},\{1,3\},\{1,4\},\{2,3\},\{2,4\},\{3,4\}$	6
3	$\{1,2,3\},\{1,2,4\},\{1,3,4\},\{2,3,4\}$	4
4	$\{1,2,3,4\}$	1
		16

Yes, set D has 16 subsets as predicted.

Using the results of this investigation, we can summarize and develop a formula to generalize the pattern.

Number of Elements	Number of Subsets
1	2
2	4
3	8
4	16
$\vdots$	$\vdots$
n	2^n

This formula seems reasonable as there are two choices for each element in the original set: either include, or exclude the element.

This pattern plants the seed for the counting techniques which we will explore further in other chapters.

EXERCISES

Exercise 2.1. Let $A := \{1, 2, 3, 4, 6, 12\}$, $B := \{2, 3, 5, 7, 11\}$ and $U := \{1, 2, 3, 4, 5, 6, 7, 8, 9, 10, 11, 12\}$

a) Draw a Venn diagram to represent the sets

b) List the elements of $A \cap B$

c) Use your answer from part b) to list the elements of $(A \cap B)^c$

d) List the elements of A^c

e) Use your answer from part d) to list the elements of $A^c \cup B$

Exercise 2.2. Complete the following.

a) List the elements of the following set. $\{x \mid x = 4n, -3 \le n \le 2, n \in \mathbb{Z}\}$

b) Write the following set in set-builder notation. $\{0, 3, 6, 9, 12\}$

Exercise 2.3. Construct a truth table for the following statement.

NOT (P OR Q) AND Q.

P	Q	P OR Q	NOT (P OR Q)	NOT (P OR Q) AND Q
T	T			
T	F			
F	T			
F	F			

3

WHOLE NUMBER

3.1 Representation of whole numbers

Whole numbers consist of the counting numbers together with 0. Our number system offers several helpful features, including a 0 and place value. Historically, the Mayan numeration system introduced a symbol for 0. Some historic number systems such as Roman numerals had neither a 0 nor a place value. The Babylonian system used a place value of 60 (similar to the relationship between seconds, minutes and hours), and the Mayans had a modified place value (base 20 and 18 combined). Our system uses base 10 for place values which makes modeling and calculating very manageable.

As students are exposed to larger numbers as they move through the grades (hundreds, thousands, millions and beyond), they discover the organization of our place value system. Students are expected to move readily among words, standard notation and expanded notation.

The number $67\,102\,345$ (equivalent to $\underbrace{67}_{millions}\,,\,\underbrace{102}_{thousands}\,,\underbrace{345}_{units})$ in standard form can be expressed in words as 'sixty-seven million, one hundred two thousand, three hundred forty-five'. (If you won a major lottery this would one of the lines on your check.) The commas shown in the number have been used to separate the millions from the thousands and the thousands from the units. The number is read as number of millions, number of thousands and then number of units.

Example 3.1.1. *Write* $67,102,345$ *in expanded form.*

▶ *Solution.* This number can be written in expanded form to show the value of each digit. We can leave out the 0 but we need to be careful of the place value as we move in this case, from the hundred thousands to the thousands.

Expanded Form
60,000,000
7,000,000
100,000
2,000
300
40
5
Total   67,102,345

◄

Changing from expanded from to standard from is generally regarded as more challenging as students need to be careful of missing place values requiring a 0.

Example 3.1.2. *Write* $20,000,000 + 3,000,000 + 50,000 + 2000 + 400 + 8$ *in standard form.*

► *Solution.* It is helpful to choose a set of blanks to complete the standard form. In this case, there are 7 blanks after the first digit since there are 7 zeros after the 2.

2 _, _ _ _ , _ _ _

We need to position the other digits so that the number of places to the right of the digit corresponds to the number of zeros in the value of the digit.

23, _ _ _ , _ _ _
23, _ 5 _ , _ _ _
23, _ 52 , 4 _ 8

We use zeros in the place values that are missing in the expanded form.

23, 052, 408

This gives twenty-three million, fifty-two thousand, four hundred eight.

Using addition, we have the following alternate solution.

Expanded Form	
	20,000,000
	3,000,000
	50,000
	2,000
	400
	8
Total	23, 052, 408

◀

3.2 Order and Rounding of Whole Numbers

As students practise communicating whole numbers through standard form, expanded form and words, they can also use base 10 blocks to represent them. Base ten blocks are available for ones, tens, hundreds and thousands. After communication and representation of whole numbers, students are ready to compare and order whole numbers.

Example 3.2.1. *Order the following numbers from least to greatest:*
21 245, 23 442, 21 542, and 2145.

▶ *Solution.* The smallest number has the least number of digits making 2145 the smallest of the list as it has only four digits (up to thousands), while the other three numbers include ten thousands. The largest number in this set is 23 442 since it has the largest number of thousands, 23 thousand. Of the two remaining numbers, 21 245 and 21 542 both have 2 in the ten thousand and 1 in the thousand place but they differ in the hundreds place. Therefore, $21245 < 21542$.

This gives the numbers in order from least to greatest as: 2145, 21 245, 21 542, 23 442. ◀

ROUNDING WHOLE NUMBERS

A skill related to ordering whole numbers is the skill of rounding. This also relies on a strong understanding of place value. To round a number, we first identify the place value to which we are asked to round. Then we consider *only* the digit immediately to the right of this place. If the digit to the right is 5 or higher, then we round the digit under consideration up 1. If the digit to the right is 4 or less, then we leave the digit under consideration the same. Generally, digits to the left of the rounding place remain the same (see example 3.2.3 as an exception) and digits to the right of the rounding place become zeros.

Example 3.2.2. *Round the number* 12 682 *to the nearest hundred.*

▶ *Solution.* Identify the 6 as the digit in the hundreds place 12 $\textcircled{6}$82.
Is 12 682 closer to 12 600 or 12 700?
Immediately to the right of the 6 is a 8 so we will round the 6 up to a 7 to obtain
12 682 ≈ 12 700.   ◀

Example 3.2.3. *Round the number* 413 962 *to the nearest hundred.*

▶ *Solution.* Identify the 9 as the digit in the hundreds place 413 $\textcircled{9}$62.
Is 413 962 closer to 413 900 or 414 000?
Notice that there is the possibility of changing the digit immediately to the left of the
9 in this situation. Immediately to the right of the 9 is a 6 so we will round the 9 up
but that involves rounding the thousands up to a 4. This gives 413 962 ≈ 414 000 as the
rounded answer.   ◀

| **3.3** | Operations With Whole Numbers |

Base 10 blocks are helpful for developing the skills of adding, subtracting, multiplying
and dividing whole numbers. The following block representations are used.

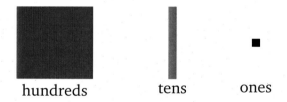

hundreds   tens   ones

ADDING WHOLE NUMBERS

To add two whole numbers, we can display the two numbers and then use regrouping,
(starting with the unit column) to find the sum.

Example 3.3.1. *Evaluate* 256 + 157.

▶ *Solution.*

$$
\begin{array}{r}
256 \\
+157 \\
\hline
\textbf{Total} \quad 413
\end{array}
$$

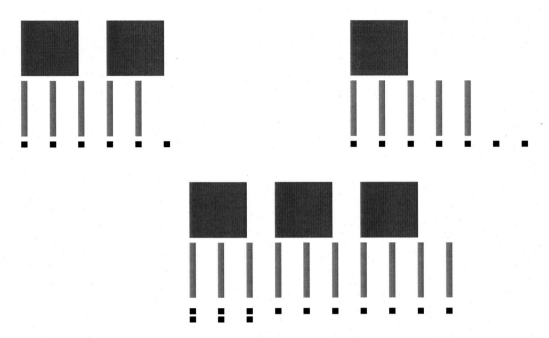

We have 13 ones, so we can trade 10 ones for another 10, leaving us with 3 ones.

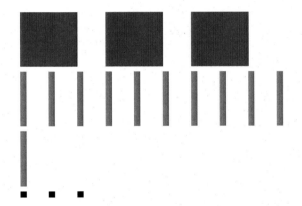

That will give use 11 tens, so we can trade 10 tens for another 100, leaving us 1 ten.

Answer

Illustrating $256 + 127 = 413$. ◄

SUBTRACTING WHOLE NUMBERS

For subtraction of whole numbers with base ten blocks, the 'take away' approach works well. We can display the first number and then regroup as necessary, to take away the second number (starting with the ones)

Example 3.3.2. *Evaluate* $243 - 125$.

▶ *Solution.*

$$
\begin{array}{r}
243 \\
-125 \\
\hline
\textbf{Result} \quad 118
\end{array}
$$

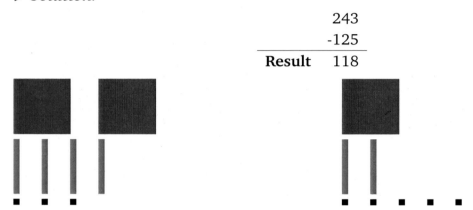

We start again with the ones position. Since we only have 3 ones in 243 and we need to take away 5 ones, we can trade one ten for 10 more ones. This gives 2 hundreds, 3 tens, and 13 ones.

Now we can take away 125 by removing 5 ones, 2 tens and 1 hundred. This will leave us with 118.

Answer

Illustrating $243 - 125 = 118$.

◄

MULTIPLYING WHOLE NUMBERS

Multiplication of a single digit by a two or three digit number can be carried out by letting the single digit represent the number of groups and the other number the content of the groups. Again regrouping allows students to determine the product.

Example 3.3.3. *Evaluate* 24×3.

► *Solution.* To show 24 x 3, we can make 3 groups of 24 by treating multiplication as repeated addition.

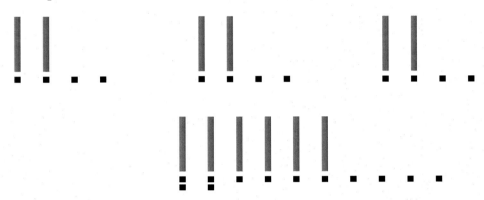

We have 12 ones, so we can trade 10 ones for another ten, leaving us with 2 ones and 7 tens.

Answer

Illustrating $24 \times 3 = 72$.

◄

Multiplication of a two digit number by another two digit number is possible through an array in which the two original numbers represent the frame of the array and the product is displayed by tiling the array with blocks

Example 3.3.4. *Evaluate* 14×12.

▶ *Solution.*

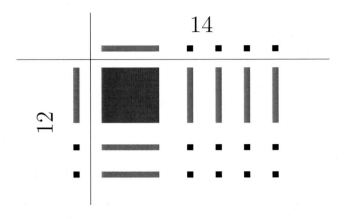

Answer $14 \times 12 = 100 + 60 + 8 = 168$ ◀

DIVISION OF WHOLE NUMBERS

To perform division of a two or three digit number by a single digit, we can display the dividend and then make equally sized groups, the number of which is based on the single digit. As students make the groups, they need to regroup, starting with the largest place value.

Example 3.3.5. *Evaluate* $76 \div 3$.

▶ *Solution.*
We display 76 with 7 tens and 6 ones.

Since we are dividing by 3, we want to make three equally sized groups, in this example with 2 tens and 2 units.

One remaining tile.   *3 equal groups*

This leaves us with one ten that we can trade for 10 ones. At this stage, we have the following.

Ten remaining tiles.   *3 equal groups*

Answer

Final   *3 equal groups*
tile

We now have 3 groups of 25, remainder 1, illustrating $76 \div 3 = 25$ remainder 1. ◀

3.4   Mental mathematics, and Properties of Whole Numbers

There are various properties of whole numbers and their operations that assist with mental mathematics.

The commutative property applies to addition and multiplication and it allows students to add or multiply two numbers in either order. Adding $2 + 19$ has the same result as adding $19 + 2$. Similarly, 5×7 gives the same result as 7×5. This property can be shown using manipulatives such as counters, cubes, or base ten blocks.

The associative property extends the commutative property to 3 or more numbers and still applies to addition and multiplication. To add or multiply a list of numbers, the associative property allows us to reorganize the numbers into compatible pairs of addition or multiplication.

Compatible pairs make a number that simplifies calculations, such as a multiple of 10, or 100.

Example 3.4.1.

$$45 + 52 + 55 + 48 + 24$$
$$= (45 + 55) + (52 + 48) + 24$$
$$= 100 + 100 + 24$$

Example 3.4.2.

$$2 \times 12 \times 5$$
$$= (2 \times 5) \times 12$$
$$= 10 \times 12$$
$$= 120$$

The distributive property exists for multiplication over addition and multiplication over subtraction. It allows us to break up a multiplication question into simpler multiplications that can be evaluated without a calculator. The distributive property is also a fundamental property in algebraic reasoning (more to come in chapter 7).

Example 3.4.3. *Evaluate* 4×123.

▶ *Solution.*

$$4 \times 123$$

$$= 4 \times (100 + 20 + 3)$$

$$= (4 \times 100) + (4 \times 20) + (4 \times 3)$$
$$= 400 + 80 + 12$$
$$= 492$$

The distributive property is illustrated between the second and third lines. ◄

Example 3.4.4. *Evaluate* 5×99.

▶ *Solution.*

$$5 \times 99$$

$$= 5 \times (100 - 1)$$

$$= (5 \times 100) + (5 \times (-1))$$
$$= 500 - 5$$
$$= 495$$

The distributive property is used between the second and third lines, this time using multiplication over subtraction. ◄

EXERCISES

Exercise 3.1. Model the following with pictures of base ten blocks. Include the paper pencil calculation

a) $45 + 78$ 　　　　　　　　　　　　　b) $32 + 62$

Exercise 3.2. Model the following with pictures of base ten blocks. Include the paper pencil calculation

a) $3 \times 24 = 72$, show 24 + 24+ 24 　　　b) $5 \times 12 = 60$

Chapter 4

FACTORS AND MULTIPLES

FACTORS

What does it mean to say that 6 is a factor of 24?

- 24 is divisible by 6, with remainder 0

- 6 divides evenly into 24

- There exists a natural number n such that $6n = 24$

Some numbers have an abundance of factors but others have only a few factors. For example, 72 has 12, and 360 has 24 factors. A prime number is a natural number that has only two distinct factors (namely, 1 and itself). For example, 2, 3, 5, 7, 11, and 13 are all prime numbers. Notice that 2 is the only even prime number. There is an infinite number of prime numbers; in other words, there is no largest prime number. Many mathematicians have endeavoured to find a formula to predict prime numbers but this problem has generally remained unsolved. Researchers are interested in finding large prime numbers as they are helpful in making codes that protect people when they enter personal information such as a credit card number in online banking or shopping.

How can we decide if a number is prime? Do we have to check to see if the number is divisible by any of the numbers less than that number? The good news is that we only need to check to see the number can be divided by any of the prime numbers less than or equal to its square root. For example, the square root of 101 is about 10. The prime numbers less than 10 are 2, 3, 5, and 7. To decide if 101 is prime or not, we check to see if 101 divides by 2, 3, 5 or 7. Since 101 is not divisible by 2, 3, 5 or 7, it is prime.

Its only factors are 1 and 101.

A number that has more than two factors is called composite. Every composite number can be uniquely written as a product of prime numbers using a factor tree. To make a factor tree, start with any two factors of a number and then continue to decompose the number until prime numbers are reached.

Example 4.1.1. *Construct a factor tree to show the prime factors of 24 .*

▶ **Solution.** *One*   ▶ **Solution.** *Two*   ▶ **Solution.** *Three*

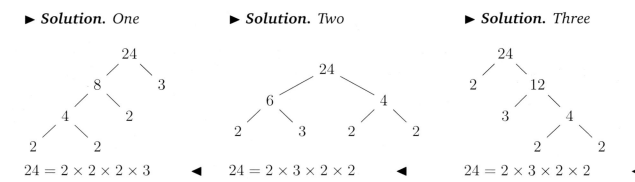

$24 = 2 \times 2 \times 2 \times 3$ ◀ $24 = 2 \times 3 \times 2 \times 2$ ◀ $24 = 2 \times 3 \times 2 \times 2$ ◀

4.2   Divisibility rules

Divisibility rules are handy tricks for students and teachers to carry in their mathematical toolbox to help them determine the factors of a given number. To say that m is divisible by n means that m divides evenly by n. In other words, n is a factor of m.

To test whether a number is divisible by 2, 5, or 10, we only need to check the last digit. If the last digit is 0, 2, 4, 6, or 8, then the number is even (divisible by 2) and if the last digit is 0 or 5, then the number is divisible by 5. By putting those two rules together, a number is divisible by 10 if the last digit is 0.

Example 4.2.1. *The number* 123, 456 *is divisible by 2 but not by 5 or* 10 *while the number* 123, 450 *is divisible by 2,* 5 *and* 10.

The rules for divisibility by 3 and by 9 are similar in that we need to add the digits of the number. If the sum of the digits is divisible by 3, then so is the original number. If the sum of the digits is divisible by 9, then so is the original number. Note that if a number is divisible by 9, then it is also divisible by 3 but the converse is not true.

Example 4.2.2. *For the number* 123, 456 *the sum of the digits is* $1 + 2 + 3 + 4 + 5 + 6 = 21$. *(Optionally) repeating the sum of digits* $2 + 1 = 3$, *which is divisible by 3 but not by 9. Therefore the number* 123, 456 *is divisible by 3 but not divisible by 9.*

To check whether a number is divisible by 4, we look at the number formed by the last two digits. To test for divisibility by 8, we look at the number formed by the last three digits. These rules are a result of the fact that 100 is divisible by 4 and 1000 is divisible by 8.

Example 4.2.3. $123,456$ *The number formed by the last two digits (56) is divisible by 4 so the number $123,456$ is divisible by 4. The number formed by the last three digits (456) is divisible by 8 (using long division) so the number $123,456$ is also divisible by 8.*

A number is divisible by 6 if and only if it is divisible by both 2 and 3. $123,456$ is divisible by 6 since it is divisible by both 2 and 3. Similarly, a number is divisible by 12 if and only if it is divisible by both 4 and 3. The number $123,456$ is divisible by both 3 and 4, making it divisible by 12.

The divisibility test for 7 involves more calculations. Take off the last digit, double it, and subtract it from the number. Repeat this process until a number is obtained that is recognizably divisible by 7 or not.

Example 4.2.4. *Determine whether or not 123456 is divisible by 7.*

▶ *Solution.*

original number	last digit removed	last digit	last digit doubled	subtract
123456	12345	6	12333	
12333	1233	3	6	1227
1227	122	7	14	108
108	10	8	16	-6

These calculations will sometimes result in a negative number. Since -6 is not divisible by 7, neither is the number $123,456$. ◀

There is a three step calculation to decide if a number divides evenly by 11. First, add every other digit starting with the ones position. Secondly, add every other digit starting with the tens position. Thirdly, take those two answers and subtract the smaller from the greater. If the result is divisible by 11, ex 0, 11, 22, 33, ..., then so is the original number.

DIVISION BY 11

To determine whether or not a number is divisible by 11, in sequence *from the right* alternately subtract then add the digits. Repeat this pattern until a single digits occurs. If the result is 0, the original number is divisible by 11.

Example 4.2.5. *Determine whether or not 1358016 is divisible by 11.*

▶ *Solution.* Digit Calculations: $6 - 1 + 0 - 8 + 5 - 3 + 1 = 0 \rightarrow 1358016$ is divisible by 11. ◀

DIVISIBILITY SUMMARY

Divisor	Method	Conclusion
2	Divide the last digit by 2.	If the remainder is 0, then 2 is a divisor of the original number.
3	Add the digits. Repeat until there is one digit.	If this digit divides by 3, then 3 is a divisor of the original number.
4	Divide the last two digits by 4.	If the remainder is 0, then 4 is a divisor of the original number.
5	the last digit is 0 or 5.	If yes, then 5 is a divisor of the original number.
6	Use divisors 2, and 3.	If both are divisors, then 6 is a divisor of the original number.
7	Multiply the last digit by 2 and subtract it from the number. Repeat until a number is obtained that is recognizably divisible by 7.	If yes, then the original number is divisible by 7.
8	Divide the last three digits by 8.	If the remainder is 0, then 8 is a divisor of the original number.
9	Add the digits. Repeat until there is one digit.	If this digit is a 9, then 9 is a divisor of the original number.
10	Check the last digit.	If the digit is 0, the original number is divisible by 10.
11	*Beginning on the right*, alternately subtract then add the digits in sequence. Repeat this pattern until a single digits occurs.	If the result is 0, the original number is divisible by 11.

4.3   Greatest Common Factor

The teachers of class 6A (28 students) and of class 6B (32 students) would like to divide each class to equal groups of students. What is the greatest number of students that the teachers can place in each group?

The factors of 28 are 1, 2, 4, 7, 14, 28.
The factors of 32 are 1, 2, 4, 8, 16, 32.

The common factors are 1, 2, and 4 and the greatest common factor (GCF) is 4. Therefore, the teachers can place 4 students in each group. There will be 7 groups in class 6A and 8 groups in class 6B.

The above example illustrates the listing method, which helps to practice math facts and to develop the concept of common factors. However, it can be time-consuming and risky for large numbers because a factor could be overlooked.

Factor trees can handle larger numbers and have the advantage of only requiring two factors begin the factorization.

Example 4.3.1. *Determine* GCF $(72, 80)$

▶ *Solution.*

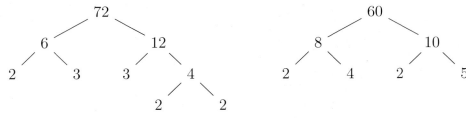

Once the factor trees are made, compare the prime factorization of the two numbers, identify the common prime factors, and then multiply them together.

$$72 = \circled{2} \times 3 \times 3 \times \circled{2} \times \circled{2}$$
$$80 = \circled{2} \times \circled{2} \times \circled{2} \times 2 \times 5$$

They both have three factors of 2 in their prime factorization so GCF $(72, 80) = 2 \times 2 \times 2 = 8$ ◄

There are two other methods, reversed division and the Euclidean algorithm, which can process even larger numbers as the factor trees can become cluttered for numbers in the hundreds or thousands. Both of these methods rely on division skills and facts.

For reversed division, we divide the two numbers by common prime factors until they have no further factors in common. The following example shows how to find the GCF $(120, 180)$ using reversed division. We divide both numbers by 2 as long as possible, then we continue with 3 and 5. The process stops when we reach 2 and 3 as they have no further common prime factors. To find the GCF, we multiply the common prime factors on the left side of the diagram.

Example 4.3.2. *Determine* GCF $(120, 180)$ *using reversed division.*

▶ *Solution.*

$$
\begin{array}{c|cc}
2 & 120 & 180 \\
2 & 60 & 90 \\
3 & 30 & 45 \\
5 & 10 & 15 \\
& 2 & 3
\end{array}
$$

$$\text{GCF}\,(120, 180) = 2 \times 2 \times 3 \times 5 = 60$$

◄

The Euclidean algorithm is named after Euclid, a mathematician known as "The Father of Geometry" who made contributions to geometry and number theory. He discovered that the GCF (n, m) where $n > m$ is the same as the GCF (m, r) where r is the remainder when n is divided by m.

The algorithm repeats a process of division until a remainder of zero is reached. At each stage of the algorithm, the previous divisor and remainder are used to make a new division statement.

Example 4.3.3. *Determine* $\text{GCF}\,(1225, 875)$ *using the Euclidean algorithm.*

► *Solution.*

number	divisor	quotient	remainder	statement
1225	875	1	350	$1225 = 1 \times 875 + 350$
875	350	2	175	$875 = 2 \times 350 + 175$
350	175	2	0	$350 = 2 \times 175 + 0$

The greatest common factor shows up as the second to last remainder (which is also the last divisor).

In this case, $\text{GCF}\,(1225, 875) = 175$. ◄

4.4   Lowest Common Multiple methods

Your family is hosting a barbeque and you need to go shopping for hamburgers and hamburger buns. The burgers come in packages of 8 while the buns come in packages of 6. How many packages of each should you buy to have the same number of burgers as buns? We could start with some skip counting. When we skip count, we are writing the multiples of 6 and the multiples of 8 in a pattern.

$$M_6 = \left\{ 6, 12, 18, \boxed{24}, 30, 36, 42, \boxed{48}, 54, \ldots \right\}$$

$$M_8 = \left\{ 8, \quad 16, \quad \boxed{24}, \quad 32, \quad 40, \quad \boxed{48}, \quad 56, \ldots \right\}$$

These sets are infinite (they have no end) but we already have at least one match (24). We could buy 4 packages of 6 and 3 packages of 8 to make 24 hamburgers and hamburger buns. Another possibility as we continue to study the lists is 48. There are an infinite number of common multiples. We can choose 24, 48, 72, ... depending on how many people are coming for the barbecue. We say that 24 is the lowest common multiple and we will also see this as a helpful number when we find the lowest common denominator for adding or subtracting two fractions.

The method of listing multiples is useful for numbers that are small enough for easy skip counting but the method can be time-consuming and error-risky for larger numbers. Another method is to use factor trees to obtain the prime decomposition of each number.

Example 4.4.1. *Find the LCM of 48 and 60.*

▶ **Solution.**
Factors of 48

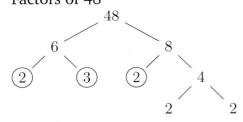

Factors of 60

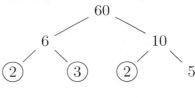

$$48 = \boxed{2} \times \boxed{3} \times \boxed{2} \times 2 \times 2$$
$$60 = \boxed{2} \times \boxed{3} \times \boxed{2} \times 5$$

To find the $LCM\,(48, 60)$, we multiply the prime factors (circled) that they have in common by the 'leftover' prime factors to get

$$LCM\,(48, 60) = \boxed{2} \times \boxed{3} \times \boxed{2} \times 2 \times 2 \times 5 = 240$$

◀

The method of using factor trees to find prime decompositions can handle large numbers but there is another method, reversed division, that can take care of even larger numbers and that can handle more than 2 numbers effectively.

Example 4.4.2. *Find* $LCM\,(36, 84, 112)$.

$$
\begin{array}{c|ccc}
2 & 36 & 84 & 112 \\
2 & 18 & 42 & 56 \\
3 & 9 & 21 & 28 \\
7 & 3 & 7 & 28 \\
  & 3 & 1 & 4
\end{array}
$$

In the first two divisions (by 2), we could divide all three numbers by 2. In the third and fourth divisions, we could only divide two of the numbers. Reversed division ends when there are no common factors for the numbers, taken three at a time or two at a time (other than 1). To find the LCM, we now multiply all factors on the left side and the bottom of our reversed division chart.

$$LCM\,(36, 84, 112) = 2 \times 2 \times 3 \times 7 \times 3 \times 1 \times 4 = 1008$$

EXERCISES

Exercise 4.1. Complete the following.

a) Make a factor tree for 36.

b) Make a factor tree for 84.

c) Use the prime factorization of 36 and 84 from steps a) and b) to determine the GCF (36, 84)

d) Use the prime factorization of 36 and 84 from steps a) and b) to determine the LCM (36, 84)

Exercise 4.2. Use reversed division to determine

a) the GCF (36, 84)

b) the LCM (36, 84).

Exercise 4.3. Test the number 31108 for divisibility by 3, 4, 7 and 11.

Exercise 4.4. Determine whether 1009 is prime or composite. Show any necessary steps.

Exercise 4.5. Use the Euclidean algorithm to find GCF (775, 1075)

5 INTEGERS

5.1 Representation and Ordering of Integers

The integers are a natural extension of the whole numbers. The integer set, $\mathbb{Z}$, includes 0, and positive and negative natural numbers. They are needed to be able to represent items such as: as cold temperatures, financial debt, measurements below sea level or downward travel.

The letter $\mathbb{Z}$, stands for the German word 'zählen', meaning 'to count'.

When students enter the world of integers, they start exploring the meaning and representation of integers. For example, a positive integer, such as +5, could represent a gain of 5 dollars, an increase in temperature by 5 degrees, a movement left or down. On the other hand, a negative integer, such as -5, could mean a loss of 5 points, a drop in the stock market of 5 points, a descent in an elevator of 5 floors. Helpful manipulatives to develop the concept of integers include:

- counters with two different colours

- number lines

- thermometers

- transparent base ten blocks with two different colours.

Example 5.1.1. *Earn 5 dollars, spend 5 dollars. The net result is 0 dollars. All cash was spent.*

ORDERING INTEGERS

The next step in developing understanding of integers is to arrange then in order. Students already have already practised ordering positive integers and they can easily compare a positive integer to a negative integer. To compare two negative integers, the number line is the most effective as it clearly demonstrates that the negative integers are a mirror image of the positive integers.

Example 5.1.2. *Using a number line show* $(-4) < (1)$.

▶ *Solution.*

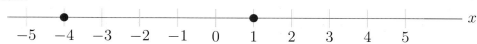

◀

Example 5.1.3. *Using a number line show* $1 < 4$.

▶ *Solution.*

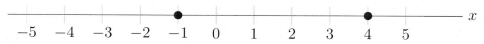

◀

Example 5.1.4. *Arrange the numbers* $3, -1, -2, 4$ *in the order lowest to highest using*

a) a number line

b) counters

▶ *Solution.*

USING A NUMBER LINE

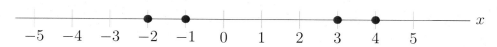

USING COUNTERS

Stones, in the original order.

Stones, arranged in order.

In order, lowest to highest, $-2, -1, 3, 4$. ◀

5.2 Operations with integers

Once students have practised comparing integers, they are prepared to carry out operations with integers. We can use two different colours of counters for positive and negative numbers, and then model the four operations using two different methods: using counters, and using a number line.

OPERATIONS USING COUNTERS

An important principle when using counters is the zero pair principle. This states that the same number of positive and negative counters adds to zero.

With counters, we can display counters to represent each number in the question, using the zero principle to remove each pair of a positive and a negative, and then organize and count the remaining counters.

THE SIMPLEST ZERO PAIR

$$\oplus\ominus = 0$$

OPERATIONS USING A NUMBER LINE

When we use the number line to model the operations, $+, -, \times$, we will use *straight* arrows to show our travels right or left along the line. Motion to the right is defined as the positive direction, and motion to the left is defined as the negative direction.

For addition on a number line we start at zero, move to the first number, and then move right to add a positive number, or left to add a negative number.

ADDITION

Adding two positive numbers together will give another positive number. The following examples show that adding two negatives gives another negative (like spending more money, or the temperature becoming increasingly colder). When adding two numbers with opposite signs the result may be negative or a positive, depending on whether there are more negatives or positives.

Example 5.2.1. *Evaluate* $6 + 2$ *using counters*

▶ *Solution.*

$$6 + 2 = 8.$$

◀

Example 5.2.2. *Evaluate* $(-6) + (-2)$ *using counters*

▶ *Solution.*

$$(-2) + (-6) = -8$$

◀

Example 5.2.3. *Evaluate* $(-6) + 2$ *using counters*

▶ *Solution.*

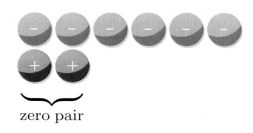

zero pair

$$(-6) + 2 = -4$$

◀

SUBTRACTION

Showing subtraction using counters is more of a challenge with integers. For a question like $(+7) - (+3)$ which is the same as $7 - 3$, we could simply display 7 positive counters and remove 3 positive counters leaving 4 positive counters. For $(+7) - (-3)$, we cannot remove 3 negative counters since we have only positive counters to begin. This is where the zero pair principle can be used. Since we need 3 negative counters to remove, introduce 3 zero pairs of counters. The net total of counters is still 7. (This would be true regardless of the number of zero pairs introduced.)

USING COUNTERS

7

$7 \underbrace{+ 3 + (-3)}_{\text{zero pair}}$

$7 - (-3)$

$= 10$

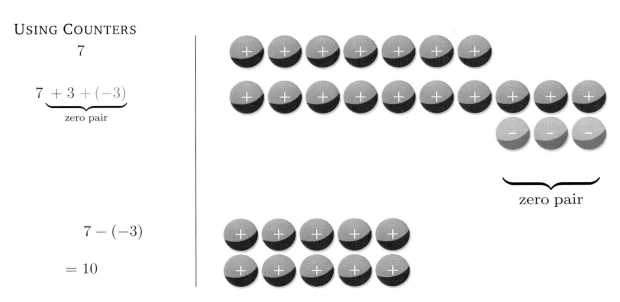

Between every list of integers, there is an addition sign. It is recommended to rewrite any subtractions in the form of an addition. The result is that subtracting any integer is the same as adding its opposite. Now, we can write

$$(7) - (-3)$$
$$= (7) + (+3)$$
$$= 10$$

Similarly, we can rewrite

$$(-7) - (-3) = (-7) + (+3)$$
$$(-7) - (+3) = (-7) - (+3)$$

Example 5.2.4. *Evaluate* $(-7) - (-3)$ *using counters*

▶ **Solution.** Remove 3 negative stones.

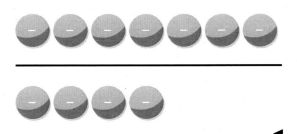

▶ **Solution.** Add the opposite of −3

Example 5.2.5. *Evaluate* $(-7) - (+3)$ *using counters*

▶ **Solution.** Add −7 and −3.

◀

▶ **Solution.** Introduce 3 zero pairs, and then remove +3.

◀

MULTIPLICATION

Multiplication of two integers can be illustrated well using repeated addition, as long as one of the numbers is positive. A question like $(3) \times (4)$, or simply 3 x 4, can be easily modeled by displaying 3 groups of 4 positive counters, or 4 groups of 3 positive counters. Using a number line, a student can start at 0 on the number line and make 3 forward paths of 4, or 4 forward paths of 3 to reach +12.

If we have one negative and one positive integer in a multiplication question, then select the positive number to represent the number of groups. For instance, to model $3 \times (-4)$, we can display 3 groups of 4 negative counters, while to model $4 \times (-3)$, we can use 4 groups of 3 negative counters. To complete these multiplications using a number, 3 backwards paths each of size 4 will model 3 x (-4), while 4 backwards paths each of size 3 will model (-3) x 4. These examples could be compared to the temperature decreasing the same interval over a several days or to a shopper making several purchases of the same dollar amount.

To illustrate the product of two negative integers using counters, we will need to be more creative. We can think of removing a certain number of groups of counters in order to handle this situation. In order to model $(-3) \times (-4)$, we can think of *removing* 3 groups, each with 4 negative counters. (This is the reverse of the earlier suggestion of writing subtraction questions as addition questions.)

$$0 + (-3) \times (-4)$$
$$= 0 - \left[\underbrace{(3) \times (-4)}_{3 \; groups \; of \; -4} \right]$$
$$= 0 - (-12)$$
$$= 0 + (12)$$
$$= 12$$

This requires that we have some counters to start with. Using the zero principle, we can begin with the same number of positive and negative counters. (Although the initial number of positive and negative counters must be the same, net total of 0, at least 12 will be required.) After removing 3 groups of 4 negative counters, we are left with 12 positive counters. This model can be used to explain why the multiplication of two negative integers gives a positive integer. This is harder to compare to a real life situation but one possibility is the removal of debt. If you have 3 kind friends, to each of whom you owe $4 and who each do not require you to pay back the debt, then you have in a sense gained 12 free dollars!

A number line could be used but still requires rewriting the question to have one positive number.

DIVISION

The number line does not handle division as well as the other operations, however, counters are still handy for most division problems with integers. As in multiplication, we can strive to use a positive number to represent the number of groups. So for (-10) divided by 2, we can display 10 negative counters and then share them among two equally sized groups, giving 5 negative counters in each group. In the case of (-10) divided by (-2), we can still use 10 negative counters, but this time we make groups of size 2, giving us 5 groups. The modeling of 10 divided by 2 can involve making groups of size 2 or making 2 groups; in either model, the answer is shown to be positive 5. The case of 10 divided by (-2) is very difficult to model because how can we make groups of negative counters when we have positive counters to start and how can we make negative two groups.

5.3 Properties of Integers

The set of integers has the same commutative and associative properties for addition and multiplication as do the whole numbers. They also have the distributive property of multiplication over addition.

Using the commutative and associative properties, we can reorganize a list of integers to add all the positive numbers, all the negative numbers, and then add those two answers.

Example 5.3.1. *Evaluate,* $(-2) + (-4) + 7 + (-3) + 8 + 2$

▶ *Solution.*

$$(-2) + (-4) + 7 + (-3) + 8 + 2$$
$$= \underbrace{7 + 8 + 2}_{positives} + \underbrace{(-2) + (-4) + (-3)}_{negatives}$$
$$= 17 + (-9)$$
$$= 8$$

◀

We can reorder the multiplication factors in order to place 'compatible' numbers together, such as powers of 10, $(-2) \times (-5) = 10$, in the following example.

Example 5.3.2. *Evaluate,* $(-2) \times 4 \times (-5) \times (-3)$

▶ *Solution.*

$$(-2) \times 4 \times (-5) \times (-3)$$
$$= [(-2) \times (-5)] \times [4 \times (-3)]$$
$$= 10 \times (-12)$$
$$= -120$$

◀

The distributive property of multiplication over addition can allow us to break down a multiplication question into two simpler multiplication questions that could be handled with mental mathematics.

Example 5.3.3. *Evaluate,* $-2 \times (-49)$.

▶ *Solution.* -49 rounds to -50 giving the substitution option $-49 = 1 - 50$.

$$-2 \times (-49)$$
$$= -2 \times (1 - 50)$$
$$= -2 \times 1 + (-2) \times (-50)$$
$$= -2 + 100$$
$$= 100 - 2$$
$$= 98$$

◄

IDENTITY NUMBERS

Integers, like whole numbers, have 0 as the identity for addition, and 1 as the identity for multiplication. The integers also offer an additive inverse property in that each integer has an opposite integer such that when it is added to its opposite, the result is 0. For example, 2 and (-2) are additive inverses, or more commonly, opposite integers. Added together the sum is zero, in this case forming two zero pairs.

ZERO PAIRS

EXERCISES

Exercise 5.1. Model the following integer operations using pictures of positive and negative counters.

a) $(-9) + 5$

b) $(-3) \times 6$

Exercise 5.2. Model the following integer operations using a number line.

a) $(-7) + 4$

b) $3 \times (-5)$

Exercise 5.3. Complete the following.

a) Give a numerical example to show the associative property of multiplication of integers. Show LS and RS calculations.

b) Explain using an integer model (counters, money or a pattern) why the product of two negative integers is a positive integer.

c) Give a numerical example to show that the property of additive inverses exists over the integers.

Chapter

6

FRACTIONS, DECIMALS AND PERCENT

6.1   Representation and Order of Fractions

The journey through rational numbers is similar to that of the whole numbers and integers in that students move from representation to order to operations of the numbers. Fractions developed out of a need to represent a part of a whole, a probability or a proportion of people, or objects with a given characteristic. To represent fractions, we can use circles or rectangles divided into equally sized pieces or manipulatives such as fraction circles, fraction towers or fraction strips.

Congruent rectangles or circles with equal areas of shading can serve to model equivalent fractions. For instance, a rectangle divided into 3 equal pieces with 2 shaded and 1 unshaded can illustrate $\frac{2}{3}$. If the same rectangle is further divided into 6 equal pieces, then there are now 4 shaded pieces and 2 unshaded to represent $\frac{4}{6}$. Similarly, a rectangle divided into quarters with 1 quarter shaded can represent $\frac{1}{4}$ and if this rectangle is further divided into eighths, then $\frac{2}{8}$ can now describe the shaded portion.

Example 6.1.1. *Show* $\frac{2}{3} = \frac{4}{6}$*.*

▶ *Solution.*

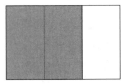 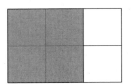

◄

Example 6.1.2. *Show* $\frac{1}{4} = \frac{2}{8}$*.*

47

▶ *Solution.*

◀

Other manipulatives to develop the concept of equivalent fractions include fractions circles or fraction towers which generally feature denominators of 1, 2, 3, 4, 6, 8, 10, 12 For instance with the fraction circles, 3 sixths, 4 eighths, 5 tenths or 6 twelfths can be superimposed on the half circle to show that they all have the same area and they are all equivalent to one half. With the fraction towers (interlocking rectangular prisms), 1 quarter cube can be placed beside 2 eighth cubes or 3 twelfth cubes to show that they all have the same length and all represent equivalent fractions.

Once students practise equivalent fractions with diagrams and concrete manipulatives, they can observe the pattern of producing an equivalent fraction by multiplying or dividing the numerator and the denominator by the same number. The skill of multiplying the numerator and denominator by the same number is helpful in setting up equivalent fractions with a common denominator to compare, add or subtract fractions. The skill of dividing both the numerator and the denominator by the same numbers is necessary to express a fraction in lowest terms.

The rectangle and circle models are also useful to illustrate how to change a mixed fraction to an improper. In the following example, the first diagram illustrates an improper fraction $\frac{11}{6}$ and the second diagram models a mixed fraction $1\frac{5}{6}$.

These diagrams can help to develop a method for changing between improper fractions (ideal for calculations) and mixed fractions (helpful for final answer).

To change a mixed fraction to an improper, we take the denominator times the whole number plus the numerator to calculate the new numerator and keep the same denominator.

In this example, the calculation $(6 \times 1) + 5 = 11$ gives the numerator of the improper fraction.

To change an improper fraction to a mixed fraction, we divide the numerator by the denominator: the quotient is the whole number, the remainder is the numerator, and the denominator remains the same. In this example, 11 divided by 6 equals 1 remainder 5, giving us $1\frac{5}{6}$ as the mixed fraction.

COMPARING FRACTIONS

To compare fractions, we can sometimes use the relative positions of two fractions on a number line between 0 and 1. For instance, $\frac{1}{6}$ is greater than $\frac{1}{7}$ since a sixth of a pizza is larger than a seventh. Similarly, $\frac{9}{10}$ is greater than $\frac{8}{9}$ since $\frac{9}{10}$ is $\frac{1}{10}$ away from 1 whole while $\frac{8}{9}$ is $\frac{1}{9}$ away from 1 whole; in other words, $\frac{9}{10}$ is closer to 1 than is $\frac{8}{9}$. For more difficult cases, we need to model the fractions with manipulatives (fraction circles or fraction towers) or establish a common denominator to compare equally sized pieces as shown in the following examples.

Example 6.1.3. *Compare $\frac{5}{8}$ and $\frac{2}{3}$ using fraction circles.*

▶ *Solution.*

Figure 6.1.1: Original fractions

Figure 6.1.2: With a common denominator of 24

Using a common denominator of 24, we have $\frac{5}{8} = \frac{15}{24}$ and $\frac{2}{3} = \frac{16}{24}$, showing $\frac{5}{8} < \frac{2}{3}$. ◀

Example 6.1.4. *Determine which fraction is larger, $\frac{3}{7}$ or $\frac{2}{5}$.*

▶ *Solution.* Denominators of 5 and 7 are not generally provided for fraction manipulatives. Using the lowest common denominator of 35, we have $\frac{3}{7} = \frac{3 \times 5}{7 \times 5} = \frac{15}{35}$ and $\frac{2}{5} = \frac{2 \times 7}{5 \times 7} = \frac{14}{35}$, showing $\frac{3}{7} > \frac{2}{5}$. ◀

6.2	Operations with Fractions

ADDITION AND SUBTRACTION OF FRACTIONS

In order to complete addition or subtraction of fractions, a common denominator is required so that we can add or subtract equally sized pieces. The following examples show a possible progression from addition/subtraction of simple fractions to addition/subtraction of mixed fractions. Fractions can be added or subtracted in the mixed fraction form but as the fifth example demonstrates, regrouping may be necessary with subtraction of mixed fractions.

Example 6.2.1. *Evaluate* $\frac{7}{10} - \frac{3}{10}$.

▶ *Solution.*

$$\frac{7}{10} - \frac{3}{10}$$

$$= \frac{4}{10} \qquad \text{already has a common denominator already}$$

$$= \frac{2}{5} \qquad \text{reduce}$$

◀

Example 6.2.2. *Evaluate* $\frac{3}{4} + \frac{2}{5}$

▶ *Solution.*

$$\frac{3}{4} + \frac{2}{5}$$

$$= \frac{3 \times 5}{4 \times 5} + \frac{2 \times 4}{5 \times 4} \qquad \text{20 is the lowest common denominator}$$

$$= \frac{15 + 8}{20} \qquad \text{write the common denominator as 'common'}$$

$$= \frac{23}{20} \qquad \text{simplify}$$

$$= 1\frac{3}{20} \qquad \text{the mixed fraction}$$

◀

Example 6.2.3. *Evaluate* $\frac{5}{9} - \frac{1}{6}$.

▶ *Solution.*

$$\frac{5}{9} - \frac{1}{6}$$

$$= \frac{5 \times 2}{9 \times 2} - \frac{1 \times 3}{6 \times 3} \qquad \text{18 is the lowest common denominator}$$

$$= \frac{10 - 3}{18} \qquad \text{write the common denominator as 'common'}$$

$$= \frac{7}{18} \qquad \text{simplify}$$

◀

Example 6.2.4. *Evaluate* $2\frac{1}{4} + 1\frac{5}{6}$.

▶ **Solution.** [Method 1]
$$2\frac{1}{4} + 1\frac{5}{6}$$
$$= 2\frac{3}{12} + 1\frac{10}{12} \quad \text{12 is the lowest common denominator}$$
$$= 3\frac{13}{12} \quad \text{simplify}$$
$$= 4\frac{1}{12} \quad \text{reduce}$$
◀

▶ **Solution.** [Method 2]
$$2\frac{1}{4} + 1\frac{5}{6}$$
$$2 + \frac{1}{4} + 1 + \frac{5}{6} \quad \text{separate into the four terms}$$
$$= 2 + 1 + \frac{3}{12} + \frac{10}{12} \quad \text{12 is the lowest common denominator}$$
$$= 3 + \frac{13}{12} \quad \text{simplify}$$
$$= 4 + \frac{1}{12} \quad \text{reduce}$$
$$= 4\frac{1}{12} \quad \text{reduce}$$
◀

Some students may prefer to use a common denominator by multiplying the two original denominators together. This method will always produce a common denominator (24 in the above example) but may require additional simplification of the final answer.

Example 6.2.5. *Evaluate* $3\frac{1}{3} - 1\frac{4}{5}$.

▶ **Solution.** [Method 1]
$$3\frac{1}{3} - 1\frac{4}{5}$$
$$= 3\frac{5}{15} - 1\frac{12}{15} \quad \text{15 is the lowest common denominator}$$
$$= 2\frac{20}{15} - 1\frac{12}{15} \quad \text{'borrow' an extra } \frac{15}{15} \text{ from the first fraction}$$
$$= 1\frac{8}{15} \quad \text{simplify}$$
◀

▶ *Solution.* [Method 2] Begin with improper fractions.

$$3\frac{1}{3} - 1\frac{4}{5}$$

$$= \frac{3 \times 3 + 1}{3} - \frac{1 \times 5 + 4}{5} \qquad \text{write both fractions in improper from}$$

$$= \frac{10}{3} - \frac{9}{5} \qquad \text{simplify}$$

$$= \frac{10 \times 5}{3 \times 5} - \frac{9 \times 3}{5 \times 3} \qquad \text{15 is the lowest common denominator}$$

$$= \frac{50 - 27}{15} \qquad \text{simplify}$$

$$= \frac{23}{15} \qquad \text{reduce}$$

$$= 1\frac{8}{15} \qquad \text{reduce}$$

◀

This second method is more common but can result in large numerators making the calculations more challenging, perhaps even 'requiring' a calculator.

MULTIPLICATION OF FRACTIONS

To explore multiplication of fractions, students can begin with a whole number multiplied by a fraction, such as $12 \times \frac{1}{4}$, which can be interpreted as sharing 12 objects among 4 equal groups and taking one of those groups to give $12 \times \frac{1}{4} = 3$. Similarly, $10 \times \frac{2}{5}$ can be interpreted as sharing 10 objects among 5 equally sized groups and then taking 2 of those groups to give $10 \times \frac{2}{5} = 4$. What observations can students make from these examples?

Example 6.2.6. *Using counters, show that $12 \times \frac{1}{4} = 3$ i.e. Share 12 counters equally among 4 groups.*

▶ *Solution.*

◀

Example 6.2.7. *Using counters, show that $10 \times \frac{2}{5} = 4$ i.e. Share 10 counters equally among 5 groups, and then determine the number of counters for two groups combined.*

▶ *Solution.*

We can achieve the answer in example **6.2.6** by writing both numbers as fractions, multiplying the numerators, and then the denominators.

$$\frac{12}{1} \times \frac{1}{4} = \frac{12 \times 1}{1 \times 4} = 3$$

In example **6.2.6**,

$$\frac{10}{1} \times \frac{2}{5} = \frac{10 \times 2}{1 \times 5} = 4$$

Can we extend this principle to a proper fraction times a proper fraction?

We can if the fractions are first written as improper fractions.

Consider the array in the first example below, formed by shading 3/5 of a rectangle in one direction (3 columns) and 1/3 in the other direction (1 row). The double shaded portion is 3/15 (purple) which is the same answer that we obtain by 3/5 x 1/3 = 3/15 through multiplication of numerators and denominators.

Example 6.2.8. *By shading a rectangular array, show that $\frac{3}{5} \times \frac{1}{3} = \frac{1}{5}$*

▶ *Solution.*

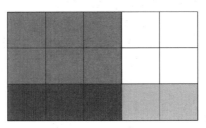

The area of the common region is $\frac{3}{15} = \frac{1}{5}$. ◀

Example 6.2.9. *Evaluate $2\frac{1}{4} \times 1\frac{2}{3}$*

▶ *Solution.* $2\frac{1}{4} \times 1\frac{2}{3}$ ◀

$$= \frac{9}{4} \times \frac{5}{3} \qquad \text{improper form for both fractions}$$

$$= \frac{45}{12} \qquad \text{simplify}$$

$$= \frac{15}{4} \qquad \text{reduce}$$

$$= 3\frac{3}{4} \qquad \text{proper fraction}$$

DIVISION OF FRACTIONS

The investigation of division of fractions can also start with a whole number divided by a simple fraction. For example, 2 pizzas divided into eight slices each requires students to determine the number of slices, $\frac{1}{8}$ pieces, that can fit into 2 wholes. Using 2 circles divided into fourths, there are 8 such pieces in 2 wholes. The situation of 2 divided by 2/3 is similar in that students can divide 2 circles into thirds and count how many groups of 2/3 are present to find an answer of 3. What pattern can students discover from these examples?

Example 6.2.10. *Using a circle diagram show that* $2 \div \frac{1}{8} = 16$.

▶ *Solution.*

◀

Example 6.2.11. *Using a circle diagram, evaluate* $2 \div \frac{2}{3}$.

▶ *Solution.*

Each piece is $\frac{2}{3}$'s of a full circle. There are three pieces.

◀

These examples suggest that to divide two fractions, we need to multiply the first fraction by the *reciprocal* of the second. Consider the following examples.

Example 6.2.12. *Evaluate* $\frac{7}{8} \div \frac{5}{12}$.

▶ *Solution.*

$$\frac{7}{8} \div \frac{5}{12}$$
$$= \frac{7}{8} \times \frac{12}{5} \quad \text{invert the second fraction and then multiply both fractions}$$
$$= \frac{84}{40} \quad \text{simplify}$$
$$= \frac{21}{10} \quad \text{reduce}$$
$$= 2\frac{1}{10} \quad \text{proper fraction}$$

Example 6.2.13. *Evaluate $2\frac{3}{4} \div 1\frac{2}{3}$.*

▶ *Solution.*

$$2\frac{3}{4} \div 1\frac{2}{3}$$

$$= \frac{11}{4} \div \frac{5}{3} \qquad \text{improper fractions}$$

$$= \frac{11}{4} \times \frac{3}{5} \qquad \text{invert the second fraction and then multiply both fractions}$$

$$= \frac{33}{20} \qquad \text{simplify}$$

$$= 1\frac{13}{20} \qquad \text{proper fraction}$$

◀

6.3　Fractions and Decimals

As students develop skills in fractions, they develop parallel skills in decimal representation and operations. Base 10 blocks (with a shift in place value from the whole numbers) and decimal paper (square grids divided into tenths, hundredths or thousandths) are valuable manipulatives in representing decimals. These manipulatives can show the relationship between fractions and decimals, and can compare decimals. For example, consider the decimals 0.3, 0.29 and 0.30. Using decimal paper divided in tenths, the student can shade 3 columns to represent 0.3 on one square. Similarly, using decimal paper divided into hundredths, the student can shade 30 squares (3 columns of 10) to show 0.30. The decimal paper model therefore demonstrates the equivalence between 0.3 and 0.30 which connects with the equivalence of fractions $\frac{3}{10}$ and $\frac{30}{100}$.

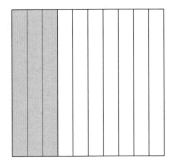 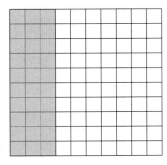

Figure 6.3.1: Illustration of 0.3　　　Figure 6.3.2: Illustration of 0.30

The decimal paper can also demonstrate that $0.3 > 0.29$.

Base ten blocks can be used to model decimal operations similar to the method presented with whole numbers in chapter 3.3 but with a 'shift' in representation. The flats, the longs and the small cubes can now represent wholes, tenths and hundredths respectively (instead of 100, 10, 1). The following examples illustrate addition and multiplication of decimals.

Example 6.3.1. *Evaluate* $2.56 + 1.75$ *using base 10 blocks.*

▶ *Solution.*

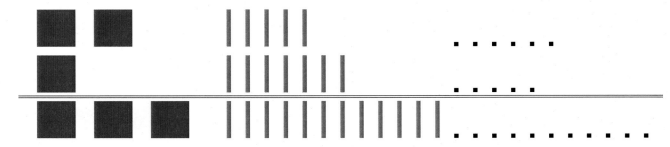

We have displayed 3 wholes, 12 tenths and 11 hundredths. We can trade 10 hundredths for another tenth and 10 tenths for another whole to give 4 wholes, 3 tenths and 1 hundredth totalling or 4.31.

◀

Example 6.3.2. *Evaluate* 0.24×4 *using base 10 blocks.*

▶ *Solution.*

$$\boxed{0.96}$$

We have displayed 8 tenths and 16 hundredths. We can trade 10 hundredths for another tenth to give us 9 tenths and 6 hundredths or 0.96. ◀

The decimal squares help to demonstrate how to change a decimal into a fraction by writing the number of shaded squares as the numerator and the total number of squares as the denominator. For instance, $0.3 = \frac{3}{10}$, $0.29 = \frac{29}{100}$ and $0.299 = \frac{299}{1000}$. In general, we can change a decimal into a fraction by writing the decimal part as the numerator and a power of 10 as the denominator to represent the last digitâĂŹs place value. For example, $0.24 = \frac{24}{100} = \frac{6}{25}$ since the 4 is in the hundredths place. Note that the fractions can be reduced to simplest terms.

If a fraction's denominator is a factor of 10, 100, or 1000, then it can be readily changed into a decimal by first writing the fraction as an equivalent fraction with a denominator of 10, 100 or 1000. For example, $\frac{16}{25} = \frac{64}{100} = 0.64$ while $\frac{2}{125} = \frac{16}{1000} = 0.016$. However, if the denominator is not a factor of 10, 100 or 1000, then long division can be used to change the fraction into a decimal. We take the numerator (with zeros added after the decimal) as the dividend and the denominator as the divisor. The following example shows how long division can be used to change a fraction into a decimal.

Example 6.3.3. *Write $\frac{5}{12}$ in equivalent decimal form.*

▶ *Solution.*

$$
\begin{array}{r}
0.4166 \\
12 \overline{\smash{)}5.0000} \\
-48 \\
\hline
20 \\
-12 \\
\hline
80 \\
-72 \\
\hline
80 \\
-72 \\
\hline
8
\end{array}
$$

We finish the long division once the decimal ends, or shows a repeating pattern. In this case, we have $0.4166\ldots$ where the 6 repeats infinitely. We can write the decimal as $0.41\overline{6}$ with a line over the 6 indicating that it repeats. ◀

REPEATING DECIMALS WRITTEN IN FRACTION FORM

Example 6.3.4. *Convert $2.3\overline{45}$ to an equivalent fraction.*

▶ *Solution.*
Let $x = 2.345454545\ldots$

Multiply both sides by a power of 10 to result in the decimal occurring *after* the first repeating pattern.
$1000x = 2345.454545\ldots$

Multiply both sides of the original equation by a power of 10 to result in the decimal occurring *before* the first repeating pattern.
$10x = 2.345454545\ldots$

Now subtract the two equations to eliminate the repeating pattern.

$$1000x = 2345.454545\ldots$$
$$10x = 23.454545\ldots$$

$$990x = 2322$$
$$x = \frac{2322}{990} = 2\frac{342}{990} = 2\frac{19}{55}$$

◀

6.4 Decimals and Percentages

Decimals can be readily converted to a percentage by multiplying by 100. Conversely, to change a percentage to a decimal, we divide by 100. Much information is presented to us in the form of a percentage, such as sales, taxes, interest rates, but we usually need a decimal form in order to perform operations. The following examples of percent problems illustrate the relationship between decimal and percent.

Example 6.4.1. *Calculate as required.*

a) *A sweater valued at $ 49.96 is on sale at 25% off the price. What are the discount, and the sale price?*

b) *A student earned 27 marks out of a possible 30 marks on a test. What percentage did the student receive?*

c) *The sale price of a barbecue marked down by 30% was $ 147.98. What was the original price of the barbecue*

▶ **Solution.**

a) To find the discount, we first change 25% to 0.25 by dividing by 100. Then we multiply $49.96 \times 0.25 = 12.49$ so the discount is $ 12.49. To find the sale price, we subtract the discount from the original price 49.96 - 12.49 = $ 37.47 Another possibility, if the question requires only the sale price, is to calculate 75% of the price by multiplying $0.75 \times 49.96 = 37.47$. If the sale is 25% off the price, then the customer pays 100 - 25 = 75% of the price.

b) To calculate what percentage one number is of another, we divide the two numbers and multiply by 100. $(27 \div 30) \times 100 = 0.90 \times 100 = 90\%$. The student received 90% on the test.

c) We need to work backwards to find the original price of the barbecue. If the sale is 30% off, then the sale price represents 100 - 30 = 70% of the price.

70% of the price is $ 147.98
1% of the price is 2.11
100% of the price is $ 211.40

We can also solve this problem by changing 30% to its decimal equivalent 0.30 and then dividing 147.98 by 0.70 to get $ 211.40

◀

6.5　Ratios, proportions and rates

Fractions provide one method of communicating a ratio, which is a comparison between two quantities. The ratio may also be expressed using a colon or the word 'to'. For instance, the ratio of boys to girls in a class is $\frac{9}{10}$, or 9:10, or 9 to 10. A practical application of ratios is finding another ratio equivalent to a given ratio which is the same process of finding an equivalent fraction. Suppose that a recipe requires 1 cup of milk for every 2 cups of flour. If we wanted to double the recipe, we would need 2 cups of milk and 4 cups of flour, since 1:2 = 2:4 or $\frac{1}{2} = \frac{2}{4}$. If we wanted to halve the recipe, we would use $\frac{1}{2}$ cup of milk and 1 cup of flour. To find an equivalent ratio, we need to multiply both numbers of the ratio by the same number.

Solving a proportion involves finding a missing value in a n equation that involves two ratios. For example, $\frac{x}{6} = \frac{12}{18}$ is a proportion which can be solved by observing that the denominators have the relationship $6 \times 3 = 18$ and by applying the same relationship to the numerators $4 \times 3 = 12$ to give $x = 4$. Not all proportions can be solved by this method however. For instance, in the case of $\frac{x}{6} = \frac{10}{15}$, 15 is not an integer multiple of 6. We can use a method of cross-multiplication to solve a proportion to get $15x = 60$ or $x = 4$. *When there is a special case where there is one fraction on each side of an equal sign*, cross-multiplication can be used when solving. This method is the basis of solving proportions for secondary school algebra, similar triangles, and trigonometry.

Rates are another concept closely connected with fractions. A rate expresses the change in one quantity for a given change in another quantity. Frequently, a rate is communicated using a unit rate, where the change in the second quantity is one unit. We might say that the price of gas is $ 1.30 per litre, the wage is $ 10.75 per hour or the speed limit is 100 km per hour. Unit rates are helpful for consumers because they allow us to compare prices effectively. To calculate a unit rate, we use division as demonstrated in the following examples.

Example 6.5.1. *In each of the following situations, determine the better buy using unit rates.*

a) *500 sheets of paper for $ 5.49 or 400 sheets of paper for $4.75*

b) *2 litres of milk for $ 2.39 or 4 litres of milk for $ 3.98*

▶ *Solution.*

a) We need to find cost of 1 litre. Using division, we have

$$\$2.39 \div 2 = \$1.195 \text{ per litre}$$
$$\$3.98 \div 4 = \$0.995 \text{ per litre}$$

Therefore, the first option is the better buy.

b) We need to find the cost of 1 sheet of paper.

$$\$5.49 \div 500 = 0.01098$$
$$\$4.75 \div 400 \approx 0.01188$$

Therefore, the second option is more economical.

◀

EXERCISES

Exercise 6.1. Find the sale price of a $ 49.96 sweater at a 25% off sale.

Exercise 6.2. Convert the following to a fraction in lowest terms. Show all work.

a) $2\frac{1}{2}\,\%$

b) $1.2565656\ldots$

Chapter 7

PATTERNS AND ALGEBRA

7.1 Number Patterns

Any sequence can be used to establish *any* pattern. The general rule is that 'any five numbers will suggest a probable continuing pattern'. In this chapter we will examine four patterns.

- arithmetic

- geometric

- quadratic

- fibonacci

ARITHMETIC PATTERNS

The arithmetic pattern you are most familiar with exists with $\mathbb{N}$, the set of natural (birthday) numbers. Each birthday is one year later than the previous. If your birthday occurred in a leap year on February 29, each February 29th birthday would be 4 years later.

A summary in a table allows an easy analysis of any set of numbers. Consider the years of the summer Olympics.

Counter	Year
1	1896
2	1900
3	1904
4	1908
5	1912

The first Olympics were held in Athens, Greece in 1896. The pattern in the table shows the pattern is 'every 4 years' there will be Olympics. The next 'expected' event would be the 1916 Olympics, however this scheduled event was cancelled due to the continuing World War.

LINEAR PATTERNS

A pattern is called 'linear' if the difference between *any* pair of consecutive terms is constant.

Differences	Counter	Year	Differences
	1	1896	
$2-1=1$	2	1900	$1900-1896=4$
$3-2=1$	3	1904	$1904-1900=4$
$4-3=1$	4	1908	$1908-1904=4$
$5-4=1$	5	1912	$1912-1908=4$

Note, a decision was made to subtract in an order that *appears* to be the opposite of the usual vertical subtraction. The order of the table can simply be reversed to be more logical.

Differences	Counter	Year	Differences
	5	1912	
$5-4=1$	4	1908	$1912-1908=4$
$5-4=1$	3	1904	$1908-1904=4$
$5-4=1$	2	1900	$1904-1900=4$
$5-4=1$	1	1896	$1900-1896=4$

Either method requires *consecutive* positions in the sequence. There are several expressions that dictate an arithmetic pattern.

- For *every* 10 students, one supervisor is required.

- For *every* hour of driving, take a 10 minute break.

QUADRATIC PATTERNS

A pattern is called 'quadratic' if the *second* difference between *any* pair of consecutive terms is constant.

Differences	Counter	Term	First Differences	Second Differences
	5	26		
$5-4=1$	4	17	$26-17=9$	
$5-4=1$	3	10	$17-10=7$	$9-7=2$
$5-4=1$	2	5	$10-5=5$	$7-5=2$
$5-4=1$	1	2	$5-2=3$	$5-3=2$

In this example, the terms are related by the formula $y = n^2 + 1$.

GEOMETRIC PATTERNS

A pattern is called 'geometric' if the ratio of *any* pair of consecutive terms is constant.

Differences	Counter	Term	Ratio of terms
	5	10000	
$5 - 4 = 1$	4	1000	$\frac{10000}{1000} = 10$
$5 - 4 = 1$	3	100	$\frac{1000}{100} = 10$
$5 - 4 = 1$	2	10	$\frac{100}{10} = 10$
$5 - 4 = 1$	1	1	$\frac{10}{1} = 10$

In this example, the terms are related by the formula $y = 10^n$.

FIBONACCI PATTERNS

A Fibonacci pattern occurs when a term is generated using two previous terms. The original Fibonacci sequence is $1, 1, 2, 3, 5, 8, 13, \ldots$ where the 10th is the sum of the 8th and the 9th term etc.

GRAPHICALLY

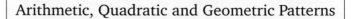

Arithmetic, Quadratic and Geometric Patterns

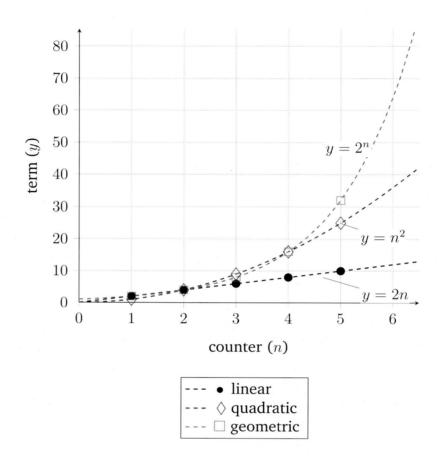

7.2   Writing and modelling algebraic expressions using algebra tiles

As shown using various models, arithmetic operations can be illustrated and completed by counting objects. For whole numbers we used the model

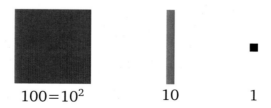

$100 = 10^2$ 10 1

Variables can also be illustrated.

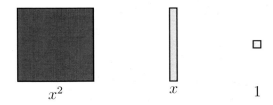

x^2 x 1

ALGEBRA TILES IN EQUATIONS

An equation can be illustrated as a balancing of two items. To maintain equality, the identical operation needs to be completed on both sides.

Example 7.2.1. *Using algebra tiles, illustrate and solve $x + 2 = 5$.*

▶ *Solution.*

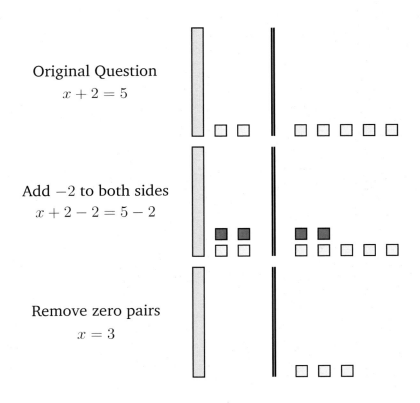

Original Question
$x + 2 = 5$

Add -2 to both sides
$x + 2 - 2 = 5 - 2$

Remove zero pairs
$x = 3$

◀

Example 7.2.2. *Using algebra tiles, illustrate and solve $2x - 3 = 1$.*

▶ *Solution.*

65

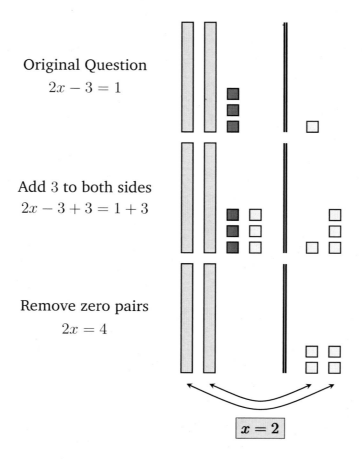

Original Question
$$2x - 3 = 1$$

Add 3 to both sides
$$2x - 3 + 3 = 1 + 3$$

Remove zero pairs
$$2x = 4$$

$$x = 2$$

Software is available at http://illuminations.nctm.org/activity.aspx?id=3482 to solve questions using algebra tiles.

7.3 Solving and modelling equations

Models can also be used for more complicated equations, however at some point, students will make similar models only in their mind.

Each of the diagrams used in this chapter were constructed using software at http://illuminations.nctm.org/activity.aspx?id=3482.

Example 7.3.1. *Using algebra tiles, solve the equation* $3x - 1 = 2x + 5$.

▶ *Solution.*

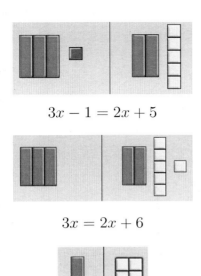

$$3x - 1 = 2x + 5$$

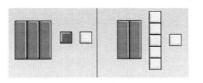

$$3x - 1 + 1 = 2x + 5 + 1$$

$$3x = 2x + 6$$

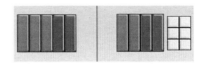

$$3x - 2x = 2x + 6 - 2x$$

$$x = 6$$

◀

Example 7.3.2. *Using algebra tiles, solve the equation* $3(x + 2) = 2(x + 4)$.

▶ *Solution.*

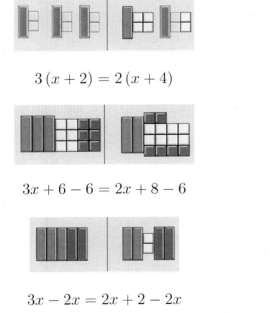

$$3(x + 2) = 2(x + 4)$$

$$3x + 6 = 2x + 8$$

$$3x + 6 - 6 = 2x + 8 - 6$$

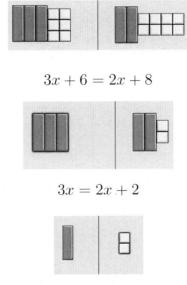

$$3x = 2x + 2$$

$$3x - 2x = 2x + 2 - 2x$$

$$x = 2$$

◀

Example 7.3.3. *Solve $\frac{1}{2}x - \frac{3}{2} = \frac{2}{3}x - 2$.*

▶ **Solution.** Deciding not to use algebra tiles, we have

$$\frac{1}{2}x - \frac{3}{2} = \frac{2}{3}x - 2$$

$$6\left(\frac{1}{2}x - \frac{3}{2}\right) = 6\left(\frac{2}{3}x - 2\right) \quad \text{Multiply both side by } LCM(2,3) = 6$$

$$3x - 9 = 4x - 12 \qquad \text{simplify (algebra tiles could now be used)}$$

$$4x - 12 = 3x - 9 \qquad \text{switch sides}$$

$$4x - 12 + 12 = 3x - 9 + 12 \quad \text{add 12 to both sides}$$

$$4x7 = 3x + 3 \qquad \text{simplify}$$

$$4x - 3x = 3x + 3 - 3x \quad \text{add } -3x \text{ to both sides}$$

$$x = 3 \qquad \text{simplify}$$

◀

7.4   Solving inequalities

An equality occurs when an equation has an equal sign between two expressions. The relationships $\neq, <, \leq, >, \geq$ are called inequalities.

An equation with $\neq$ is solved the same as an equation with $=$. The other inequality signs will reverse when an equation is multiplied or divided by a negative number.

We know $5 < 10$, but if both sides are multiplied by -2, then $-10 \not< -20 \to -10 > -20$. Similarly dividing both sides of $-10 > -20$ by -10, the result is $1 \not> 2 \to 1 < 2$.

The reverse of $\leq$ is $\geq$, and the reverse of $\geq$ is $\leq$.

Example 7.4.1. *Solve for x in the following inequality.*

$$2(x + 1) \leq 5(x - 2)$$

▶ **Solution.**

$$2(x + 1) \leq 5(x - 2)$$

$$2x + 2 \leq 5x - 10 \qquad \text{distributive property}$$

$$2x + 2 - 2 \leq 5x - 10 - 2 \quad \text{add } -2 \text{ to both sides}$$

$$2x \leq 5x - 12 \qquad \text{simplify}$$

$$2x - 5x \leq 5x - 12 - 5x \quad \text{add } -5x \text{ to both sides}$$

$$-3x \leq -12 \qquad \text{simplify}$$

$$\frac{-3x}{-3} \geq \frac{-12}{-3} \qquad \text{divide both sides by -3 and}$$

$$\text{reverse the inequality sign}$$

$$x \geq 4 \qquad \text{simplify}$$

A quick check with $x = 10 > 4$, gives $LS = 22, RS = 40$ and $LS \leq RS$ as required in the original question. ◄

GRAPHING INTERVALS

There are two basic number types, integers ($\mathbb{Z}$), and reals ($\mathbb{R}$).

Graphs of integers will have discrete points, and graphs of real number intervals will have continuous sections with an endpoint that either included or not. An endpoint that is included in the interval is graphed with a 'solid dot', and if the endpoint is not included in the interval, it is graphed with an 'open dot'.

Example 7.4.2. *Graph* $\{x \mid x \leq 2, x \in \mathbb{Z}\}$.

► *Solution.*

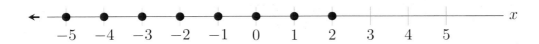

◄

Example 7.4.3. *Graph* $\{x \mid -1 \leq x < 4, x \in \mathbb{Z}\}$.

► *Solution.* The number 4 is not included.

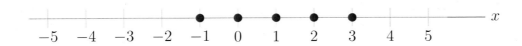

◄

Example 7.4.4. *Graph* $\{x \mid x \geq 0, x \in \mathbb{R}\}$.

► *Solution.*

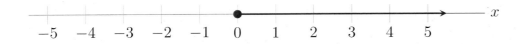

◄

Example 7.4.5. *Graph* $\{x \mid -1 \leq x < 4, x \in \mathbb{R}\}$.

▶ *Solution.*

As shown in 3.3, the product of two double digit numbers can be shown using an area structure. The question there was 14×12 and was illustrated using $(10 + 4) \times (10 + 2)$.

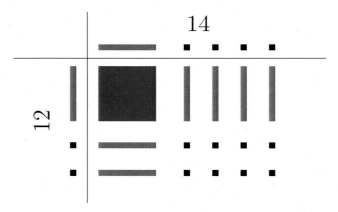

The product $(x + 4) \times (x + 2)$ is illustrated the same way with the rectangle 'value' representing x, and the square representing the value x^2.

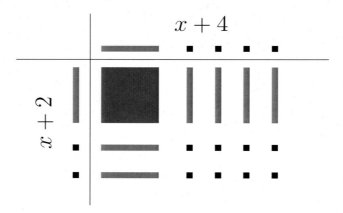

The tiles show $(x + 4)(x + 2) = x^2 + 6x + 8$

One of the required skills in mathematics is to be able to write a series of terms as a product. This process is called factoring.

Always look for a common factor first.

Example 7.5.1. *Factor* $5x + 10$.

▶ *Solution.* Both terms divide by $5 \to 5x + 10 = 5(x + 2)$. ◀

Example 7.5.2. *Factor* $x^2 + 5x + 4$.

▶ *Solution.* All three terms divide by 1, but that does not change any of the terms.

Using algebra tiles, factoring will be complete when all tiles can be arranged into a 'filled' rectangle.

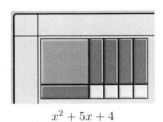
$x^2 + 5x + 4$

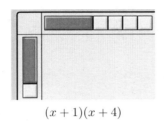
$(x + 1)(x + 4)$

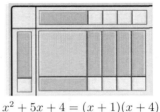
$x^2 + 5x + 4 = (x + 1)(x + 4)$

◀

Example 7.5.3. *Factor* $x^2 - x - 6$.

▶ *Solution.* All three terms divide by 1, but that does not change any of the terms.

Using algebra tiles, factoring will be complete when all tiles can be arranged into a 'filled' rectangle. Notice the introduction of 'negative' tiles.

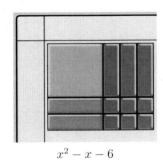
$x^2 - x - 6$

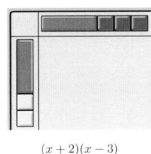
$(x + 2)(x - 3)$

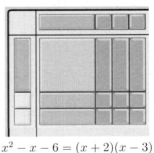
$x^2 - x - 6 = (x + 2)(x - 3)$

◀

7.6 Factoring with 'Tic-Tac-Toe' Method

FACTORING USING THE TIC-TAC-TOE FORMAT

Factoring using algebra tiles is relatively simple when all terms are positive and the x^2 term has a coefficient of 1 as shown in example 7.5.2. There is a unique method of factoring that always works for quadratic expressions in the form $ax^2 + bx + c$. This *tic-tac-toe* factoring has been modified from the *box*[1] method.

STEPS TO FACTOR THE QUADRATIC $ax^2 + bx + c$

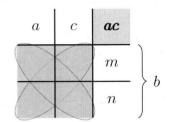

1. Common factor, if possible, but continue without it.

2. Draw a tic-tac-toe grid.

3. Enter the first coefficient in the upper left location.

4. Enter the third coefficient in the top row, middle position.

5. Multiply these numbers together and enter the answer in the upper right location.

6. The second coefficient is to be the sum of the remaining locations in the column on the right (m and n in the diagram), which are currently empty, *such that their product is also the number in the upper right position.* This requirement is the same for any quadratic factoring 'method'.

   i) List all combinations of two factors that multiply to the number in the upper right *without* using any signs.

   ii) If the upper right number is positive, add each pair of combinations. If the upper right number is negative, subtract each pair of combinations. (The order of these factors may need to be interchanged.)

   iii) Enter the two numbers that 'work' in the remaining columns on the right side. The order is not important.

7. The entries in the remaining locations are the greatest common factor of the corresponding row and column entries.

8. Check the products in each row and column (where the answers are in the top row, and the right column), and make any required sign edits. Repeat this step until all checks work.

9. The answer is 'collected' from the bottom left corner using a 'times' sign pattern with the required variable attached to the entries in the left column.

Example 7.6.1. *Factor* $10x^2 + 19x + 6$.

---

[1]Ann E, Moskal, "An Alternate Method for Factoring Quadratic Trinomials", *Mathematics Teacher* (Dec 1979): 676-7

▶ **Solution.**

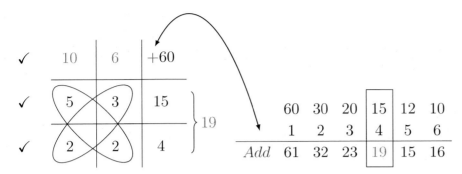

$$10x^2 + 19x + 6 = (5x + 2)(2x + 3)$$

◀

Example 7.6.2. *Factor* $6x^2 + 5x - 4$.

▶ **Solution.**

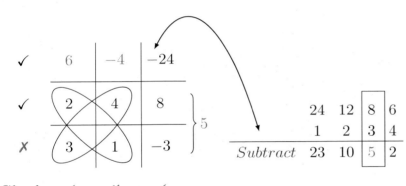

The repaired grid:

$$x^2 + 5x - 4 = (2x - 1)(3x + 4)$$

◀

EXERCISES

Exercise 7.1. Solve the following equations.

a) $3(x - 4) = 5(x + 6)$

b) $\frac{x}{5} + 8 < 2$

c) $x^2 - 7x + 12 = 0$ (Hint: Factor first)

d) $4x^2 - 25 = 0$

Exercise 7.2. Model the following using algebra tiles.

a) $2x - 5 = 3$

b) $(x + 2)(x + 4)$

c) the factoring of $x^2 + 8x + 15$

Exercise 7.3. Factor the following equations.

a) $x^2 + 6x + 5$

b) $2x^2 + 11x + 5$

c) $x^2 - 4$

d) $5x^2 - 20$

e) $4x^2 - 4x - 3$

f) $5x^2 - 12x + 4$

Chapter 8

DATA MANAGEMENT

8.1   Types of graphs

In our technological world, we are surrounded by numerical information through media and advertising. A component of numerical literacy is the ability to analyze, interpret and represent data.

Example 8.1.1. *Consider the following survey results of 20 grade students in response to the question âĂIJWhat is your favourite sport?âĂİ*

Sport	Frequency
Soccer	4
Basketball	2
Hockey	8
Volleyball	5
Other	1
Total	**20**

These results provide categorical data which is reported as frequency or percentage in each category. A pictograph or picture graph is a vivid representation of categorical data where a symbol represents a certain number.

BAR GRAPHS

A bar graph is a useful for categorical data where the height of the bars corresponds with the frequency. A bar graph may be vertical or horizontal, single or double.

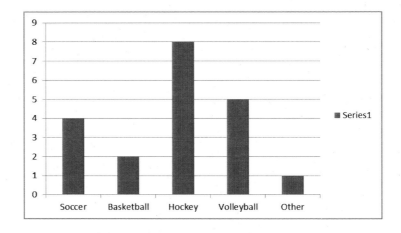

PIE GRAPHS

Yet another representation of categorical data is the circle or pie graph which connects the geometry of circle swith percentages and frequencies. In a circle graph, the area of a sector is proportional to the frequency of the category. To calculate the measure of the angle for a sector, we take the frequency of the category divided by the total frequency, then multiply by 360.

Sport	Frequency	Angle Measure
Soccer	4	72
Basketball	2	36
Hockey	8	144
Volleyball	5	90
Other	1	18
Total	20	360

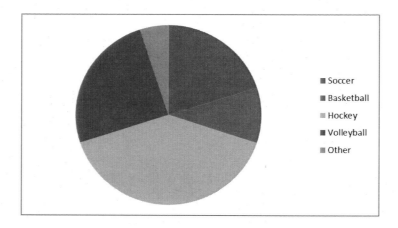

HISTOGRAM

Quantitative data, such as marks or scores, require other graphs. A histogram is similar to a bar graph except the rectangles are adjacent and they represent an interval instead of a category. For example, consider the following marks 55, 62, 67, 72, 74, 75, 76, 76, 80, 82, 82, 82, 86, 93, 94. These can be organized into 5 intervals using a bin width of 10.

Interval	Frequency
50 - 59	1
60 - 69	2
70 - 79	5
80 - 89	5
90 - 99	2

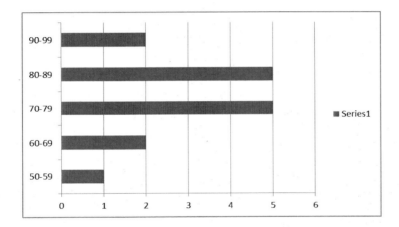

STEM AND LEAF

These marks can also be organized into a stem and leaf plot where the first digit represents the stem and the second digit, the leaf.

Stem	Leaf
5	5
6	2, 7
7	2, 4, 5, 6, 6
8	0, 2, 2, 2, 6
9	3, 4

The stem and leaf is reminiscent of a horizontal histogram where the number of leaves provides the frequency in each interval.

LINE GRAPHS

A line graph is used to show the change in a quantity over time. Time is represented on the x axis and the quantity is shown on the y axis. The quantity could be the price of a commodity, the enrollment in a program, the number of people owning a cell phone, the number of animals in a population.//

Example 8.1.2. *The following list shows the changes in enrollment at a university between 1985 and 2010.*

▶ *Solution.*

Actual Year	Year Interval	Enrollment
1985	1	1200
1990	2	1650
1995	3	1720
2000	4	1685
2005	5	1715
2010	6	1800

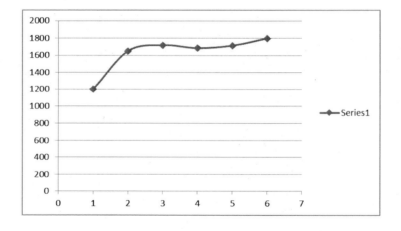

◀

SCATTERPLOTS

A scatter plot displays the relationship between two quantitative variables: an independent variable along the x axis and a dependent variable along the y axis. A scatter plot helps to visualize how a change in the independent variable affects the dependent variable. For example, a person might want to investigate the relationship between hours of study and final grade in a course or the relationship between the number of kilometers driven and the gasoline used in a particular type of car. If the scatter plot reveals a pattern between the variables, that relationship may be linear or non-linear.

Consider the following two examples.

Example 8.1.3. *Investigate the relationship between hours of study and final grade in a course given the following data.*

Time spent on video games (hours/week)	Final mark - high school math course (%)
20	65
5	90
12	77
25	52
2	98
11	75
14	6
8	65

► *Solution.*

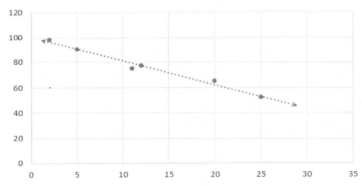

There is a moderate, negative, linear relationship between the weekly number of hours on video games and the final mark. As the number of hours on video games increases, the mark decreases. ◄

Example 8.1.4. *Investigate the relationship between the number of kilometers driven and the gasoline used in a particular type of car given the following data.*

Number of years since purchase (years)	Value ($)
1	12000
2	9800
3	7600
4	5900
5	4500

▶ *Solution.*

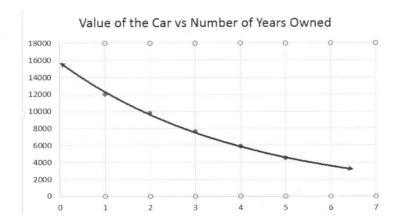

There is a non-linear relationship between the value of the car and the age of the car. ◀

8.2 Mean, Median, and Mode

Measures of central tendency or averages are used to describe quantitative data. The mean (our common notion of average) is obtained by adding all the numbers and divide by the number of numbers. For example, the mean for the list of marks in the last example of 8.1 is

$$\frac{55 + 62 + 67 + 72 + 74 + 75 + 76 + 76 + 80 + 82 + 82 + 82 + 86 + 93 + 94}{15} \approx 77.1$$

The median is the middle number of the data set when the numbers are arranged in ascending order. In the above example, the median is 76.

The mode is the most common data value which is 82 in the above set of marks.

In some cases, the median is a more accurate representation of the data than the mean because the mean is affected by extremely low or high values. For example, in the data set 4, 14, 15, 16, 16, 16, 18, 19, 20. The mean is 12 but the median is 16 which provides a more reasonable âĂİJaverageâĂİ of the data set. The mode is the type of average that is used in business to determine the most popular size, color and brand to order for customers (ex. Shoe size)

8.3 Range and Variability

The mean, median and mode, called measures of central tendency, each provide a number to represent the data set. It is also necessary to have information about the spread or variability of the data.

Example 8.3.1. *Investigate who has more consistent results given the following quiz marks for two math students.*

Student	Grades
	(%)
A	71, 73, 75, 78, 78
B	61, 71, 75, 80, 88

► *Solution.* Both students have a mean of 75 and a median of 75 but they have different ranges. Student A has a range of $78 - 72 = 6$ marks, while the range for student B is $86 - 65 = 21$ marks.

We know that the first student's marks have a narrower range.

Another calculation that tells us about the variability of the data is the standard deviation. We are interested in the average distance between each value and the mean. A chart is helpful to calculate standard deviation. First, we subtract the mean from each data value; these differences are called deviations. Secondly, we square the deviations and calculate a total. The total is divided by n, the number of data points. This answer is called the variance and the square root of the variance is the standard deviation.

Student A

	Data Value	Data Value - Mean	Square of the Deviation
	x	$x - \bar{x}$	$(x - \bar{x})^2$
	71	$71 - 75 = -4$	$(-4)^2 = 16$
	73	$73 - 75 = -2$	$(-2)^2 = 4$
	75	$75 - 75 = 0$	$(0)^2 = 0$
	78	$78 - 75 = 3$	$(3)^2 = 9$
	78	$78 - 75 = 3$	$(3)^2 = 9$
Totals	375	0	38

$$\text{Average } (\bar{x}) \quad \tfrac{375}{5} = 75$$
$$\text{Variance} \quad \tfrac{38}{5} = 7.6$$
$$\text{Standard deviation} \quad \sqrt{\text{variance}} = \sqrt{7.6} \approx 2.76$$

Student B

	Data Value	Data Value - Mean	Square of the Deviation
	x	$x - \bar{x}$	$(x - \bar{x})^2$
	61	$61 - 75 = -14$	$(-14)^2 = 196$
	71	$71 - 75 = -4$	$(-4)^2 = 16$
	75	$75 - 75 = 0$	$(0)^2 = 0$
	80	$80 - 75 = 5$	$(5)^2 = 25$
	88	$88 - 75 = 13$	$(13)^2 = 169$
Totals	375	0	406

$$\text{Average } (\bar{x}) \quad \tfrac{375}{5} = 75$$
$$\text{Variance} \quad \tfrac{406}{5} = 81.2$$
$$\text{Standard deviation} \quad \sqrt{\text{variance}} = \sqrt{81.2} \approx 9.01$$

The standard deviation for student A is less than that of student B. This shows that student A has less variable and more consistent marks than student B.

◄

EXERCISES

Exercise 8.1. Use the four step problem solving process to solve the following problems:

a) Pamela has received marks of 68, 84, 72 and 79 on her first four quizzes. What mark does she need on her fifth quiz to obtain an average of 75?

b) I am thinking of a number. When I square the number, double that answer and subtract 4, the final answer is 68.

c) Given 2, 9, 28, 65, 126, ..., find the next term in the number sequence. Explain the pattern in words.

Exercise 8.2. For the following set of marks: 85, 88, 73, 75, 76, 78, 92, 88, 83, 94

a) Calculate the mean, median and mode.

b) Calculate the variance and standard deviation by completing a table with the format

x	$x - \text{mean}$	$(x - \text{mean})^2$

c) Make a stem and leaf plot of the data.

d) Make a box and whisker plot of the data.

PROBABILITY AND COUNTING TECHNIQUES

9.1 Experimental probability

In the early elementary grades, students soon become familiar with such terms as "very probably" (such as, snow in) and "not very probably" (snow in July). Students are exposed to a continuum of similar words where percentages or fractions can be used as a measure of certainty. the percentages will be between 0% and 100% inclusive, and the fractions will be between 0 and 1.

Classroom experiments allow an opportunity to explore probability and to assign some experimental probabilities. The following examples illustrate some possible experiments with sample outcomes.

Example 9.1.1. *Students toss a pair of coins (one nickel and one dime) 20 times and record the number of HH, HT, TH, TT combinations.*

Result.

Outcome	Frequency	Experimental Probability
HH	6	$\frac{6}{20}$
HT	3	$\frac{3}{20}$
TH	6	$\frac{6}{20}$
TT	5	$\frac{5}{20}$
Total	20	1

$\Diamond$

Example 9.1.2. *Students toss a pair of dice 20 times and record the sum of the dice.*

Result.

	Sum of the faces	Frequency
	2	0
	3	1
	4	2
	5	2
	6	4
	7	4
	8	3
	9	2
	10	1
	11	0
	12	1
Total		20

◇

Example 9.1.3. *Students remove a card from a standard deck of cards, record its suit, place the card back in the deck, and repeat for a total of 20 times.*

Result.

	Outcome	Frequency
♡	Hearts	3
◇	Diamonds	7
♠	Spades	4
♣	Clubs	6
Total		20

◇

Example 9.1.4. *Students spin a spinner with five equally spaced colours (red, yellow, green, blue, purple) 20 times.*

Result.

	Outcome	Frequency
	Red	3
	Yellow	2
	Green	4
	Blue	5
	Purple	6
Total		20

As students share and compare results from these experiments, they discover that how each experiment can produce various results. Students can graph their results using a bar graph with the different outcomes on the horizontal axis and the frequency or probability on the vertical axis. Students can identify the sample space (list of possible outcomes for each experiment).

The experiments can lead to questions such as:

- How would the results change if the number of trials is increased?

- How do the results compare with student predictions?

- What events are impossible, probable or certain for the above experiments?

9.2   Theoretical probability

After enjoying various probability experiments, students can transition to theoretical probability exercises to make predictions for probability events using the formula:

Definition 2.

$$\text{\textit{Probability (event)}} = \frac{\text{Number of ways that the event can occur}}{\text{Total number of outcomes in the sample space}}$$

Example 9.2.1. *Calculate the theoretical probability for the following:*

a) Prob (tossing two heads when tossing a pair of coins)

b) Prob (tossing a face sum of 7 from a pair of dice)

c) Prob (selecting a face card when one card is drawn from a standard deck)

▶ *Solution.*

a) Sample space = {HH, HT, TH, TT}
   Prob (tossing two heads when tossing a pair of coins) = $\frac{1}{4}$.

b) There are 36 distinct outcomes when two dice are tossed.
   The following results gives a sum of 7: $1+6, 2+5, 3+4, 4+3, 5+2, 6+1$
   Prob (tossing a face sum of 7 from a pair of dice) = $\frac{6}{36} = \frac{1}{6}$.

c) There are 12 face cards (Jack, Queen, King of each suit) out of the 52 cards in a standard deck of cards.

Prob (selecting a face card when one card is drawn from a standard deck) $= \frac{12}{52} = \frac{4}{13}$.

◄

As students practice theoretical probability, the word "or" can be introduced in probability expressions. In mathematics, the word "or" is inclusive (meaning one or the other or both).

Consider the following two examples.

Example 9.2.2. *A card is drawn from a standard deck of cards. What is the probability that the card is a two or a ten?*

► *Solution.* These two events cannot happen at the same time so we can simply add their probabilities; such events are said to mutually exclusive.

$$\begin{aligned}
\text{Prob (two or ten)} &= \text{Prob (two)} + \text{Prob (ten)} \\
&= \frac{4}{52} + \frac{4}{52} \\
&= \frac{8}{52} \\
&= \frac{2}{13}
\end{aligned}$$

◄

Example 9.2.3. *A card is drawn from a standard deck of cards. What is the probability that the card is a two or a diamond?*

► *Solution.* These two events are not mutually exclusive. Since they can happen simultaneously, we need to add the probabilities and subtract their intersection, otherwise some events are counted twice.

$$\begin{aligned}
\text{Prob (two or diamond)} &= \text{Prob (two)} + \text{Prob (diamond)} - \text{Prob (two of diamonds)} \\
&= \frac{4}{52} + \frac{13}{52} + \frac{1}{52} \\
&= \frac{16}{52} \\
&= \frac{4}{13}
\end{aligned}$$

The next step in theoretical probability is to introduce two stage experiments using the word "and". For example, if a coin and a die are tossed, what is the probability of tossing a head on the coin and a 6 on the die?

A tree diagram can help to model this situation.

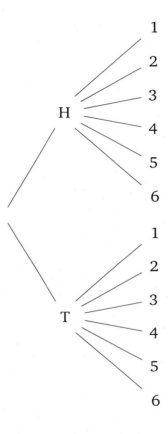

There are 12 outcomes in the sample space of tossing a coin and tossing a die.

H1, H2, H3, H4, H5, H6, T1, T2, T3, T4, T5, T6

$$\text{Prob (H6)} = \tfrac{1}{12}$$

Notice that the Prob (H) $= \tfrac{1}{2}$ and Prob (6) $= \tfrac{1}{6}$ and that the Prob (H6) $= \tfrac{1}{2} \times \tfrac{1}{6} = \tfrac{1}{12}$

This leads to an important result for probability using the word "and". We say that two events are independent if their results do not affect each other. In the above situation, the result of the coin has no effect on that of the die.

Two Independent Events
Given two independent events, A , and B, the probability of *both* events occurring is
Prob (A and B) = Prob (A) × (Prob (B).

Example 9.2.4. *Suppose a jar contains a total of 15 marbles: 5 blue marbles, 6 red marbles and 4 yellow marbles.*

a) *If two marbles are drawn with replacement (by putting back the first marble before drawing the second), what is the probability of drawing two blue marbles?*

b) *If two marbles are drawn without replacement, what is the probability of drawing two blue marbles?*

▶ *Solution.*

a) Prob (blue and blue) $= \frac{5}{15} \times \frac{5}{14} = \frac{25}{225} = \frac{1}{9}$

   Choosing a blue marble and choosing a second blue marble are independent events since we are putting the first marble back in the jar before removing the second.

b) Prob (blue and blue) $= \frac{5}{15} \times \frac{4}{14} = \frac{20}{210} = \frac{2}{21}$

   Notice that these two events are not independent. These events are dependent because the fact that the first marble is not replaced in the jar affects the sample space for drawing the second marble. After the first blue marble is removed, there are only 14 marbles (4 blue, 6 red and 4 yellow). We are still able to multiply the two probability fractions together but the second fraction is adjusted to represent that fact that the two marbles are drawn without replacement.

                                                                                            ◀

9.3 Counting Techniques

Some probability problems require more complex counting techniques to determine the total number of outcomes for the sample space and the number of outcomes for the desired event.

The Fundamental Counting Principle, which is the basis for these counting techniques, states that if there are n_1 ways of completing a first task, n_2 ways of completing a second task, $\ldots n^k$ ways of completing the kth task, then the total number of ways of completing the k tasks is the product $n_1 \times n_2 \times n_3 \times \cdots \times n_k$.

Example 9.3.1. *A restaurant is offering a special Friday deal where customers can order one appetizer, one entrée and one dessert for $14.99. There are 3 choices for appetizer (salad, soup or nachos), 3 choices for the entrée (chicken, fish or beef) and 2 choices for dessert (cake or pie). How many meals are possible?*

▶ **Solution.** The Fundamental Counting Principle tells us that there are $3 \times 3 \times 2 = 18$ possible meals. We can make a systematic list of the possible meals to confirm this number; this list will use the first two letters of each word.

(Sa, Ch, Ca), (Sa, Ch, Pi), (Sa, Fi, Ca), (Sa, Fi, Pi), (Sa, Be, Ca), (Sa, Be, Pi)
(So, Ch, Ca), (So, Ch, Pi), (So, Fi, Ca), (So, Fi, Pi), (So, Be, Ca), (So, Be, Pi)
(Na, Ch, Ca), (Na, Ch, Pi), (Na, Fi, Ca), (Na, Fi, Pi), (Na, Be, Ca), (Na, Be, Pi)

◀

Example 9.3.2. *How many*

a) *four digit numbers can be made using the digits 0 to 9 if repetition is allowed?*

b) *odd four digit numbers can be made using the digits 0 to 9 if repetition is not allowed?*

▶ **Solution.**

a) We have 10 choices for each digit except the first, where there are only 9 choices because we cannot start with a zero.

$$9 \times 10 \times 10 \times 10 = 9000 \text{ numbers}$$

The Fundamental Counting Principle is handy because a tree diagram or a systematic list has so many possibilities.

b) There are 5 choices for the last digit (1, 3, 5, 7 or 9) in order to make the number odd. There are 8 choices for the first digit (any digit except 0 or the digit already used in the last place) There are now 8 choices for the second digit and 7 choices for the third digit.
$$8 \times 8 \times 7 \times 5 = 2240$$

Note that it was necessary to consider the restrictions on the last and first digit to begin the problem.

◀

Example 9.3.3. *In how many ways can the letters of the word FRACTION be arranged? The word PARABOLA?*

▶ *Solution.* For the word FRACTION, there are 8 choices for the first letter, 7 for the second, 6 for the third and so on. This gives $8 \times 7 \times 6 \times 5 \times 4 \times 3 \times 2 \times 1 = 40320$ possible arrangements of the letters of the word fraction. For the word PARABOLA, we also have 8 letters but we have 3 A's that are identical. When the 3 A's are rearranged, a new possibility is not made. There are $3 \times 2 \times 1 = 6$ ways of arranging 3 A's so we need to take our previous answer and divide by 6. So there are $\frac{40320}{6} = 6720$ ways of arranging the letters of PARABOLA. ◀

9.4   Permutations and combinations

Example 9.4.1. *Suppose there are 8 members of a track team who are competing in an upcoming race. In how many ways can the 8 runners finish the race? In how many ways can the first, second and third place be achieved?*

▶ *Solution.* There are $8 \times 7 \times 6 \times 5 \times 4 \times 3 \times 2 \times 1 = 40320$ ways that the 8 runners can finish the race and there are $8 \times 7 \times 6 = 336$ ways that the first three places can be achieved. This a good opportunity to introduce factorial notation. For the first question in example 4, the answer can also be expressed as 8! (8 factorial). The factorial symbol, which is on most scientific calculators, tells us to multiply a number by all the natural numbers less than the number. In the second example, we could think of $8 \times 7 \times 6$ as $\frac{8!}{5!}$ ◀

Example 9.4.2. *Consider again the 8 members of the track team and their coach would like to choose 3 members to attend a special training program. In how many ways can this be done?*

▶ *Solution.* We could start with the strategy of the previous example, $8 \times 7 \times 6$, but we would be over counting since $8 \times 7 \times 6$ implies order or position for the people. Suppose A, B, C are 3 members of the team, then ABC, ACB, BAC, BCA, CAB, CBA all count as different possibilities for example 9.4.2 but they need to be counted as one possibility for this question as there is no order required. This would suggest that to calculate the number of ways in question 5, we need to divide the answer to question 4 by 6. Notice that we are choosing 3 members and $3! = 6$. For question 5, we have $\frac{8 \times 7 \times 6}{3 \times 2 \times 1} = 8 \times 7 = 56$ so there are 56 possible ways of sending 3 members to the training session. ◀

Question 9.4.2 is called a permutation which means that order is important in counting the possibilities while question 9.4.1 is called a combination. In combinations, only the resulting group is important not the order in which the objects or people are selected. We can generalize the calculations of the above two examples with two formulas, one for permutations $P(n, r)$ and one for combinations $C(n, r)$.

Permutations

$$P(n,r) = \frac{n!}{(n-r)!}$$

Combinations

$$C(n,r) = \frac{n!}{(n-r)!\,r!} \qquad \text{Also written } nCr = \binom{n}{r}$$

$n := $ the total number of people or objects

$r := $ the number of people of objects to be chosen

In the two previous examples, $n = 8$ and $r = 3$. Check that these formulas give the correct results for example 9.4.1 and 9.4.2.

9.5 Probability Questions

Combinations and permutations can be used to solve probability problems that take us beyond the tree diagrams, systematic lists and multiplication of fractions of the examples of sections 9.2.

Example 9.5.1. *There are 4 teachers and 8 students on a school yearbook committee. Three are to be chosen to make a presentation to the school.*

a) What is the probability of choosing 2 students and 1 teacher?

b) What is the probability of choosing at least one student?

▶ *Solution.*

a) We can use combinations to solve this problem since the order in which the group is chosen does not matter. Since this is a probability question, we need a combinations expression for the number of groups with 2 students and 1 teacher as well as a combinations expression for the total number of 3 member groups with no restrictions.

$$\text{Prob (2 students and 1 teacher)} = \frac{C(8,2) \times C(4,1)}{C(12,3)} = \frac{28 \times 4}{220} = \frac{28}{55}$$

◀

Example 9.5.2. *Let's return to the track team question, example 9.4.1. What is the probability of correctly guessing the top 3 winners?*

▶ *Solution.* This problem could be solved using strategies from chapter 9.2 where we multiply 3 fractions together as $\frac{1}{8} \times \frac{1}{7} \times \frac{1}{6} = \frac{1}{336}$, since we have $\frac{1}{8}$ chance of predicting the first place winner, $\frac{1}{7}$ for the second place and $\frac{1}{6}$ for the third place. We can also apply our permutations technique since order is important in this probability situation. There is only 1 way of correctly predicting the actual set of winners and there are $P(8,3)$ ways of choosing and arranging the top three winners. So the probability is $\frac{1}{P(8,3)} = \frac{1}{336}$ ◀

EXERCISES

Exercise 9.1. A coin is tossed then a die is tossed.

a) Draw a tree diagram to model this situation.

b) List the sample space.

c) Determine the probability of tossing a head and an even number.

d) Determine the probability of tossing a tail and a prime number.

Exercise 9.2. Two cards are drawn without replacement from a standard deck of cards. Calculate the probability of drawing:

a) an ace then a queen

b) an ace then a club (2 cases)

Exercise 9.3. Answer the following.

a) How many five-digit numbers can be made using the digits 0 to 9 if repetition of digit is allowed?

b) How many odd five-digit numbers can be made using the digits 0 to 9 if repetition is not allowed?

Exercise 9.4. An art club with 10 students participated in a painting contest.

a) In how many ways can first, second and third prize be assigned?

b) If four students are to be chosen to attend a painting workshop, in how many ways can this be done?

Exercise 9.5. Answer the following.

a) A jar contains 10 blue marbles and 12 red marbles. Six marbles are randomly drawn from the jar. What is the probability of drawing three blue and three red marbles?

b) If 8 coins are tossed, what is the probability of obtaining 3 heads and 5 tails?

c) If the letters of the word "FORMULA" are rearranged, what is the probability that the arrangement starts with a vowel?

Exercise 9.6. If two dice are tossed, calculate the odds in favour of tossing doubles.

10 GEOMETRY

10.1 Definitions

Buildings are constructed using angles, rectangles and other geometric shapes. Modes of transportation depend on circular wheels and controls.

Historically, geometry developed from the need to delineate property boundaries and to construct significant structures such as the Great Pyramids.

Figure 10.1.1: Great Pyramid of Giza[1]

In his geometry writing, Euclid, known as the "Father of Geometry" defined the basic building blocks of geometry and used inductive reasoning to prove many results.

DEFINITIONS

- point: the most fundamental element of geometry, is a location in space.

- line segment: the shortest connection between two points

- ray: a line segment with an initial point but no end point

- line: a line segment that extends indefinitely in both directions

---

[1]"Kheops-Pyramid" by Nina - Own work. Licensed under CC BY 2.5 via Wikimedia Commons - http://commons.wikimedia.org/wiki/File:Kheops-Pyramid.jpg#/media/File:Kheops-Pyramid.jpg

- plane: a flat surface with two dimensions (length and width).

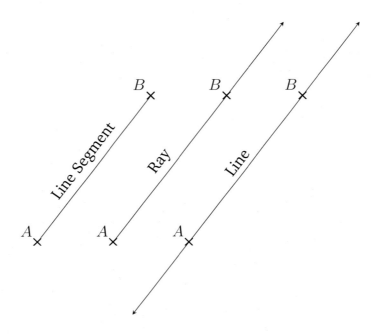

ANGLES MEASURES

Two rays that have the same beginning point enclose an angle. There are special angles measures:

- right angles (90°)

- straight angles (180°), often used in construction.

- acute angles measure less than a right angle, between 0° and 90°, such as the smaller angle between the hands of the clock at 2 o'clock.

- obtuse angles measure more than a right angle between 90° and 180°, such as the smaller angle between the hands of the clock at 6:05.

- reflex angles measure more than an obtuse angle, between 180° and 360°, such as the larger angle between the hands of the clock in each of the two previous examples.

10.2 Angle Patterns

INTERSECTING LINES

Two intersecting lines generate two angle relationships.

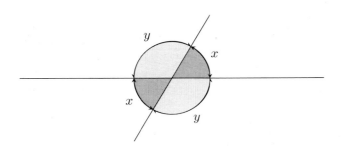

- Opposite angles are equal

- $2x + 2y = 360$
  $$\therefore x + y = 180$$

  Each consecutive pair of angles are supplementary — their measures add to $180°$.

TRANSVERSAL

A line that crosses two or more parallel lines is called a transversal. The resulting angles generate additional angle relationships.

Moving copies of the original line in the direction of the transversal shows the relationships of the angle measures.

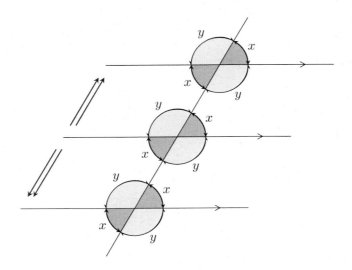

ALTERNATE ANGLES

Pairs of angles that enclosed in a Z pattern are called alternate angles and have equal measure.

CORRESPONDING ANGLES

There are four positions for an F pattern, also called corresponding angles. Corresponding angles are on the same side of the transversal and are either both above the parallel lines or both below the parallel lines. These pairs of angles are also equal in measure.

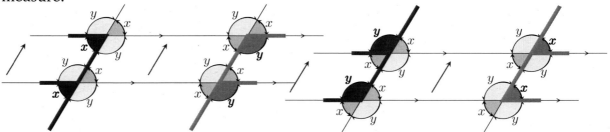

INTERIOR ANGLES

Contained between the parallel lines, and on the same side of the transversal, there are two angles that are supplementary i.e. their measures and to $180°$. These angles form a C pattern and are called co-interior angles.

Each of the above angle patterns occur when there are parallel lines and a transversal. The converse is also true. If those patterns occur, there are two corresponding parallel lines.

Example 10.2.1. *Determine the measure of the angles in the following diagram.*

$$\frac{3x + 75}{b} \Big/ \frac{a}{c}$$

$$\frac{d}{e} \Big/ \frac{2x + 45}{f}$$

▶ *Solution.* Angle c is opposite and its measure is then $3x + 75$.

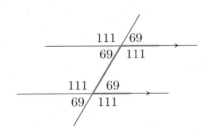

There is a 'C pattern' on the right side of the transversal giving the value of x.

$$3x + 75 + 2x + 45 = 180$$
$$5x + 120 = 180$$
$$5x + 120 - 120 = 180 - 120$$
$$5x = 60$$
$$\frac{5x}{5} = \frac{60}{5}$$
$$x = 12$$
$$2x + 45 = 69$$
$$3x + 75 = 111$$

With the remaining angle patterns we have $a = b = e = 69$ and $c = d = f = 111$.

◀

10.3   Polygons

A simple closed curve is a curve that starts and ends at the same point and does not cross over itself. It defines two regions, the interior and the exterior. A polygon is a simple closed curve that consists of line segments. The polygon is named by the number of line segments or sides that it contains, as shown in the following examples.

Name	Number of sides
Triangle	3
Quadrilateral	4
Pentagon	5
Hexagon	6
Heptagon	7
Octagon	8
Nonagon	9
Decagon	10

A polygon with all sides of equal measure is called a regular polygon.

Figure 10.3.1: The shape of a stop sign is a regular polygon

CONCAVE AND CONVEX

All regular polygons are convex. This means the line segment joining any pair of points selected inside the polygon is totally contained in the polygon. Polygons that are not convex are called concave.

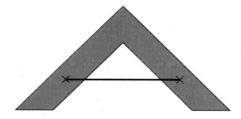

Figure 10.3.2: A chevron is a concave polygon

10.4   Types of triangles

Triangles can be classified according to sides or angles. Using classification by sides, we have

Name	Number of equal sides or angles
equilateral	3
isosceles	2
scalene	none

Classifying using angle measure, we have

- an acute triangle: all angles are acute

- a right triangle: one right angle, two acute angles

- an obtuse triangle: one obtuse angle, two acute angles

Combinations of these classifications do occur. For example, an equilateral (regular) triangle has all three angle measures of $60°$, so the triangle is also acute. A right triangle may be an isosceles triangle when the two arms of the right angle are congruent. An obtuse triangle may be scalene or isosceles.

Figure 10.4.1: A triangle that is both isosceles and obtuse

10.5 Properties of quadrilaterals

There are special quadrilaterals[2] based on the number of parallel sides, number of equal side lengths, and measure of the interior angles.

definition	parallel sides	equal side measures	angle measure
parallelogram	2 pairs	2 opposite pairs	2 equal pairs, opposite angles
rectangle	2 pairs	2 opposite pairs	90°
square	2 pairs	4	90°
rhombus	2 pairs	4	2 equal pairs, opposite angles
trapezoid	1 pair	varies	varies
kite	none	2 pairs	2 equal pairs

Some descriptions overlap. For example, a square also satisfies all other definitions.

---

[2]see https://www.mathsisfun.com/quadrilaterals.html

ADDITIONAL QUADRILATERAL PROPERTIES

Each of the quadrilaterals has additional properties. These can be developed using models and measuring, software such as GeoGebra[3], or analytic geometry. The *investigations* of various geometric properties is often an entire unit. A brief summary follows.

One of the most important additional properties is that the length of the diagonals of any rectangle or any square are always equal. This is a critical check in construction, manufacturing of doors or windows, carpet installation, etc.

The rectangle, parallelogram, rhombus and square each have diagonals that bisect each other i.e. intersect at the midpoint.

The diagonals of a square, rhombus, and the kite have diagonals that intersect at $90°$.

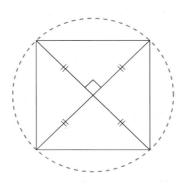

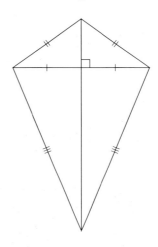

Figure 10.5.1: Diagonal properties of a
square

Figure 10.5.2: Kite properties

10.6   Angle sum of polygons

Initially, students may be asked to measure angles and to investigate the interior angle sum of various triangles. They will discover that the sum is $180°$.

The theory supporting this discovery can be proven using two parallel lines and two transversals that meet at a point on one of the parallel lines. The following diagram can be used together with the angle properties from chapter 10.2.

---

[3]http://www.geogebra.org

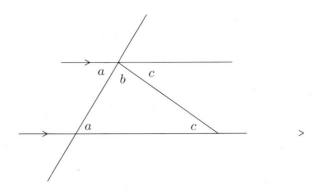

By constructing one diagonal, a quadrilateral can be divided into two triangles and so the interior angle sum of a quadrilateral is $2 \times 180 = 360°$.

Example 10.6.1. *A pentagon can be divided into 3 triangles by drawing two diagonals from one vertex. Each triangle has an interior angle sum of* $180°$ *so the pentagon has total interior angle measure of* $180 \times 3 = 540°$.

MEASURES OF INTERIOR ANGLES

In general, for a convex polygon with n sides we can draw $n - 2$ diagonals from one vertex. These diagonals divide the polygon into $n - 2$ triangles. The sum of the measures of the interior angles of a polygon with n sides is $(n - 2) \times 180°$.

For a regular polygon, the measure of each interior angle is

$$\frac{(n - 2) \times 180°}{n}$$

EXTERIOR ANGLES

Each interior angle in a polygon has one corresponding exterior angle which is supplementary to the interior angle. If x is the measure of an interior angle of a regular polygon, then the corresponding exterior angle measure is $180 - x$. If the concave polygon has n sides, then we have the following relationship, even if the polygon is not regular.

Measuring in degrees we have

$$\text{Sum of exterior angles} = 180n - \text{sum of interior angles}$$
$$= 180n - 180(n-2)$$
$$= 180n - 180n + 360$$
$$= 360$$

So the sum of the measures of the exterior angles of any polygon is always $360°$.

10.7 Tesselations

REGULAR TESSELLATIONS

Tessellation, or tiling, is the arrangement of tiles to fill a flat surface without gaps and without overlapping any tiles. For a 'regular' tessellation, all corners meet and no corner of any tile is to touch the edge of another tile. This means, at each point in the tessellation where the polygons corners meet, the total measure of the angles is $360°$.

There are only three shapes that can form these 'regular' tessellations: the equilateral triangle, square, and regular hexagon.

Example 10.7.1 (Honeycomb). *Three regular hexagons meet at each point in the tiling:* $3 \times 120 = 360°$.

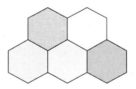

Example 10.7.2. *Four squares meet at each point in the tiling:* $4 \times 90 = 360°$.

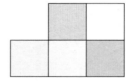

Example 10.7.3. *Six equilateral triangles meet at each point in the tiling:* $6 \times 60 = 360°$.

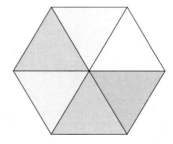

TESSELLATIONS WITH DIFFERENT POLYGONS

To make a tiling pattern of two or more different polygons, a total angle measure of $360°$ is required at each corner point.

Example 10.7.4. *Tile using four equilateral triangles and one regular hexagon meeting at each corner:* $4 \times 60 + 1 \times 120 = 360°.$

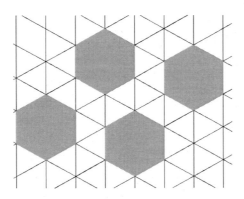

Figure 10.7.1: Corner with hexagon, six triangles

Example 10.7.5. *Tile using two octagons and one square meeting at each corner:* $2 \times 135 + 90 = 360°.$

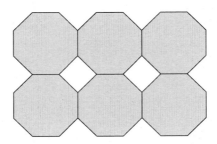

Figure 10.7.2: Corner with two octagons, one square

10.8 Prisms vs. pyramids

PRISMS

A prism is an extruded polygon where each face[4] on the sides of the extrusion is a rectangle. They are named by their 'base'.

---

[4]https://img0.etsystatic.com/036/0/5257348/il_570xN.545139374_ttpp.jpg

Figure 10.8.1: Extruder Bits

Example 10.8.1. *Using models, count the number of faces, edges, and vertices for various prisms* [5].

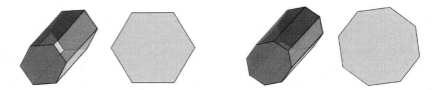

Figure 10.8.2: hexagonal and octogonal prisms

▶ *Solution.* A summary of results.

Prism	Base Edges	Faces	Vertices	Prism Edges
Triangular	3	5	6	9
Rectangular	4	6	8	12
Pentagonal	5	7	10	15
Hexagonal	6	8	12	18
⋮	⋮	⋮	⋮	⋮
n-gonal	n	$n+2$	$2n$	$3n$

◀

Notice that in each row of the chart, $F + V - E = 2$. This is an important property of polyhedrons, discovered by Euler[6].

PYRAMIDS

A pyramid is formed by joining each corner of its base to a single point. They also are named by their 'base'.

---

[5]http://www.k6-geometric-shapes.com/prisms.html
[6]http://www.math.ubc.ca/~cass/courses/m308-03b/projects-03b/wagner/Webpage.htm

Example 10.8.2. *Using models, count the number of faces, edges, and vertices for various pyamids.*

Figure 10.8.3: square and pentagonal pyramids

▶ *Solution.* A summary of results.

Pyramid	Base Edges	Faces	Vertices	Pyramid Edges
Triangular	3	4	4	6
Square	4	5	5	8
Pentagonal	5	6	6	10
Hexagonal	6	7	7	12
$\vdots$	$\vdots$	$\vdots$	$\vdots$	$\vdots$
n-gonal	n	$n+1$	$n+1$	$2n$

◀

Again notice that in each row of the chart, $F + V - E = 2$.

10.9 Platonic solids

Platonic solids are solids that have one type of regular polygon as each face and the same number of these faces meeting at each vertex. For example, a cube has six faces that are squares and there are 3 squares meeting at each vertex. There are four other Platonic solids.

The tetrahedron, also called a triangular pyramid, has 4 faces that are equilateral triangles. The octahedron with 8 faces that are equilateral triangles is considered the dual of the cube. While the cube has 6 faces and 8 vertices, the octahedron has 8 faces and 6 vertices.

The dodecahedron with 12 faces that are regular pentagons and 20 vertices is dual with the icosahedron which has 20 faces that are equilateral triangles and 12 vertices.

Example 10.9.1.

Figure 10.9.1: tetrahedron

Figure 10.9.2: cube (Hexahedron)
6 faces, 8 vertices and
12 edges

Figure 10.9.3: Octahedron
8 faces, 6 vertices and
12 edges

Figure 10.9.4: Dodecahedron
12 faces, 20 vertices
and 30 edges

Figure 10.9.5: Icosahedron
20 faces, 12 vertices
and 30 edges

Notice that $F + V - E = 2$ is still true for the Platonic solids.[7] [8] [9] [10] [11]

---

[7] http://commons.wikimedia.org/wiki/File:Tetrahedron.jpg#/media/File:Tetrahedron.jpg box "Hexahedron". Licensed under CC BY-SA 3.0 via Wikimedia Commons -

[8] http://commons.wikimedia.org/wiki/File:Hexahedron.jpg#/media/File:Hexahedron.jpg "Octahedron" by The original uploader was Cyp at English Wikipedia Later versions were uploaded by Fropuff at en.wikipedia. - Transferred from en.wikipedia to Commons.. Licensed under CC BY-SA 3.0 via Wikimedia Commons -

[9] http://commons.wikimedia.org/wiki/File:Octahedron.jpg#/media/File:Octahedron.jpg "Dodecahedron" by Created by en:User:Cyp and copied from the English Wikipedia. - not stated. Licensed under CC BY-SA 3.0 via Wikimedia Commons -

[10] http://commons.wikimedia.org/wiki/File:Dodecahedron.jpg#/media/File:Dodecahedron.jpg "Icosahedron" by Created by en:User:Cyp and copied from the English Wikipedia.This image was created with POV-Ray - en:image:poly.pov. Licensed under CC BY-SA 3.0 via Wikimedia Commons -

[11] "Icosahedron" by Created by en:User:Cyp and copied from the English Wikipedia.This image was

SEMI-REGULAR SOLIDS

When more than one type of face is used, the solid is called semi-regular. The number and type of polygons coming together are consistent for each vertex in a semi-regular solid. For example, a soccer ball (known as a truncated icosahedron) consists of 20 hexagonal and 12 pentagonal faces, with two hexagons and one pentagon meeting at each vertex.

Example 10.9.2.

Figure 10.9.6: A soccer ball: truncated icosahedron

Figure 10.9.7: A soccer ball: truncated icosahedron

The soccer ball has 32 faces, 60 vertices and 90 edges. ($F + V - E = 32 + 60 - 90 = 2$)

Another example of a semi-regular solid is a truncated icosidodecahedron. It has 62 faces (30 squares, 20 hexagons and 12 decagons), 120 vertices and 180 edges. ($F + V - E = 62 + 120 - 180 = 2$)

Both diagrams[12] were completed by Robert Webb [13].

The above two examples together with 11 other semi-regular solids make up a group of solids called the Archimedean solids, all of which are related to the Platonic solids using various geometric constructions.

---

created with POV-Ray - en:image:poly.pov. Licensed under CC BY-SA 3.0 via Wikimedia Commons -
[12] http://math.ucr.edu/home/baez/mathematical/400px-truncated_icosidodecahedron.png
[13] http://en.wikipedia.org/wiki/Stella_%28software%29 http://www.software3d.com/Stella.php

Measurement is an important part of mathematics that is used in various careers, such as construction, architecture, mechanics, engineering, fashion design. In a classroom, measurement can be introduced using non-standard units, such as paper clips or cubes as units of measurement. This allows students an opportunity to practise finding the length of their hand, desk, book, classroom, etc . . . without using rulers. For a beginner, it is easier to record a measurement as 6 cubes instead of reading the marks on a ruler.

The next step allows a student to measure length, mass, volume, etc . . . with standard units. To learn all measuring systems, it is important to know the basic units of length, mass, area, and volume. For the metric system, prefixes are used with all basic units, and multiplication or division by powers of 10. The following staircase illustrates the prefixes: milli (m), centi (c), deci (d), deca (da), hecto (h) and kilo (k) coupled with the base unit of length metre 'm'. These same prefixes can be used with any other metric base unit, such as mass (gram, g) or volume (litre, L). The staircase provides a visual/physical model for unit conversion in the metric system. In order to climb the staircase, we need to divide by 10^n. Similarly to move down the staircase we need to multiply by 10^n , where n represents the number of steps to travel from one unit to the other. The result is all digits move one decimal place to the right for each step going 'up' the stairs, and all digits move one decimal place left for each step 'down'.

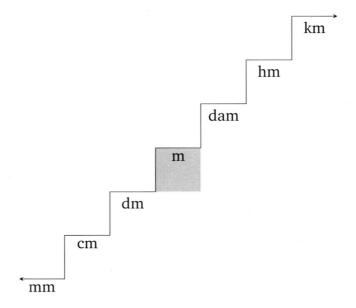

Figure 11.1.1: Stair units of length (metric)

There are applications where the conversion between units is not as simple, for example, units of time.

$$
\begin{aligned}
1 \text{ week} &= 7 \text{ days} \\
1 \text{ day} &= 24 \text{ hours} \\
1 \text{ hour} &= 60 \text{ minutes} \\
1 \text{ minutes} &= 60 \text{ seconds}
\end{aligned}
$$

There is another measuring system called the Imperial system where, for length

$$
\begin{aligned}
1 \text{ mile} &= 1760 \text{ yards} \\
1 \text{ yard} &= 3 \text{ feet} \\
1 \text{ foot} &= 12 \text{ inches}
\end{aligned}
$$

These alternate units will only be used when an application requires them. For example, in a recipe, it is common to see tablespoon or teaspoon measure. Note: 1 tbsp = 1 tsp.

All unit conversions are available in various tables on-line.
See `http://www.onlineconversion.com` or other sites.

Example 11.1.1. *Change units as stated.*

a) 2300 m, to kilometres

b) 1.6 cm, to millimetres

c) 2500 mg, to grams

d) 0.5 L, to millilitres

▶ **Solution.**

a) 2300 m = 2.300 km (divide by 1000 since we are moving 3 steps up)

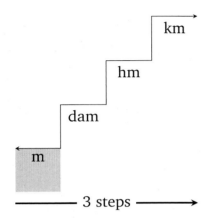

Move the digits three decimal places to the right

2300.0

   2.300

b) 16 cm = 160 mm (multiply by 10 since we are moving 1 step down)

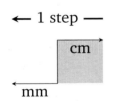

Move the digits one decimal place to the left

  16.00

160.0

c) 2500 mg = 2.5 g (divide by 1000 since we are moving 3 steps upward)

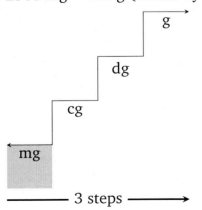

Move the digits three decimal places to the right

2500.00

   2.500

d) 0.5 L = 500 mL (multiply by 1000 since we are moving 3 steps down)

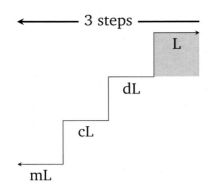

Move the digits three decimal places to the left

$$0.500$$

$$500.000$$

◀

11.2 Perimeter

The perimeter of a figure is the distance around its outside, the sum of all its exterior side lengths. Standard shapes have their own formula for perimeter.

Perimeter

Rectangle: $P = 2\ell + 2w$

$\ell : = $ length

$w : = $ width (with the same units as ℓ)

Square: $P = 4\ell$

$\ell : = $ side length

tRegular n-gon: $P = n\ell$

$\ell : = $ side length

$n : = $ the number of sides

Example 11.2.1. *Determine the perimeter of the following rectangle.*

3 cm

10 cm

▶ *Solution.* The perimeter of the rectangle is $P = 2(10) + 2(3) = 20 + 6 = 26$ cm ◀

Example 11.2.2. *Determine the perimeter of a regular pentagon with side length 4 cm.*

▶ *Solution.* The perimeter is $P = 5 \times 4 = 20$ cm. ◀

Example 11.2.3. *Determine the perimeter of the following 'rectangular' shape. It would fold to make an open box.*

3 cm

2 cm

10 cm

▶ *Solution.* The corners that are cut out do not change the perimeter. The perimeter can then be calculated from the following diagram.

7 cm

14 cm

$$P = 2\,(14) + 2\,(7)$$
$$= 28 + 14$$
$$= 42 \text{ cm}$$

◀

CIRCLE PERIMETER

For a circle, the perimeter is called the circumference (C). The formula for calculating the circumference of a circle is

Circumference of a Circle

$$C = \pi d$$
$$\text{or } C = 2\pi r$$

$\pi \approx 3.14$ (an irrational number)

$d : =$ diameter

$r : =$ radius.

The fraction approximation $\pi \approx \frac{22}{7}$ is sometimes used, but in ancient civilizations $\pi \approx \frac{333}{106}$ was used.[1] Over the the years, significant research has been dedicated to calculating more digits of its infinite decimal representation.

We can discover approximations of π in classroom activities by exploring the ratio of circumference to diameter for each circle in a collection of different sized circles.

Example 11.2.4. *Determine the circumference of the following circle with a radius of 5 cm.*

---

[1]see http://www.math.rutgers.edu/~cherlin/History/Papers2000/wilson.html 1 Kings 7:23, circa 550BC

▶ **Solution.** $C = 2\pi r$

$\qquad$ $C = 2\pi\,(5)$

$\qquad$ $C = 31.14\,\text{cm}$ $\quad$ (rounded to two decimal places)

◀

Area can be introduced using figures on graph paper, where students can count the number of squares that make up a figure. In the case of partial squares, they can estimate the area by putting together partial squares to make whole squares. Geoboardscan also be used to explore the concept of area as students count the squares formed by the pegs inside the elastic figure.

A set of rectangles on graph paper can be used to introduce the formula for the area of a rectangle. For example, a rectangle which is 2 squares by 6 squares, a rectangle that is 3 by 4 and a rectangle that is 1 by 12 all have the same area of 12 square units on graph paper. Furthermore, 2 x 6 = 3 x 4 = 1 x 12 = 12; in these three cases, the area is the product of the length times the width and the dimensions are factors of 12. The following example shows the calculation of the area of a rectangle using the formula $A = \ell \times w$.

Example 11.3.1. *Determine the area of the following rectangle.*

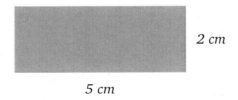

2 cm

5 cm

▶ **Solution.** $A = \ell \times w$

$\qquad$ $A = 5 \times 2$

$\qquad$ $A = 10\ \text{cm}^2$

◀

Using a cut and paste method, we can transform a parallelogram into a rectangle to explore its area. This can be done again using graph paper or geoboard figures. Notice that the length and width of the newly formed rectangle came from the base and height respectively of the parallelogram. This allows us to conclude that the area of a parallelogram equals $A = b \times h$.

Example 11.3.2. *Determine the area of the following parallelogram.*

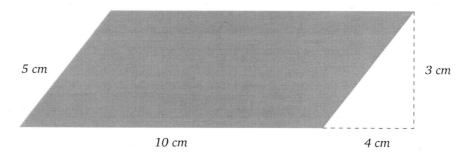

▶ *Solution.*

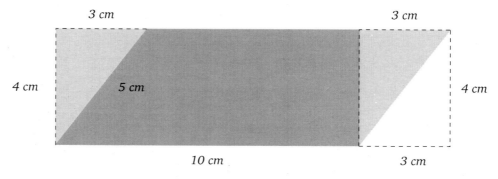

Area of rectangle: $\qquad A = \ell \times w = 10 \times 4 = 40\ cm^2$
Area of original parallelogram: $\quad A = b \times h = 10 \times 4 = 40\ cm^2$ ◀

Next, the observation that rectangles and parallelograms can both be separated into two identical triangles by constructing a diagonal, leads to the formula that the area of a triangle is half the area of a parallelogram. In other words, the formula for the area of a triangle is $A = \frac{base \times height}{2}$.

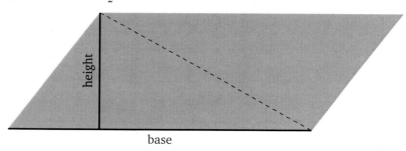

Example 11.3.3. *Determine the area of the following triangle.*

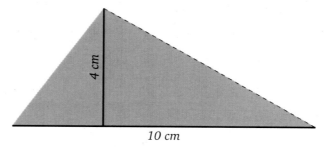

▶ *Solution.*
$$A = \frac{\text{base} \times \text{height}}{2}$$
$$A = \frac{10 \times 4}{2}$$
$$A = \frac{40}{2}$$
$$A = 20 \text{ cm}^2$$
◀

For other polygons, such as pentagons, hexagons, octagons . . . we can separate the polygon into any set of shapes and add up the area of each shape. Usually it is best to preserve the original vertices, or corners, in these shapes. Rectangles, and triangles are the usual shapes used.

Example 11.3.4. *Determine the area of the following shape*

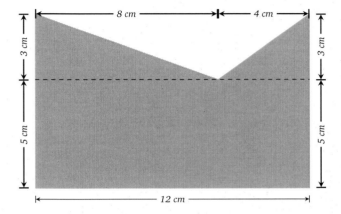

▶ *Solution.* [1] The area of the composite shape is the sum of the area of the rectangle and the area of each of the two triangles.

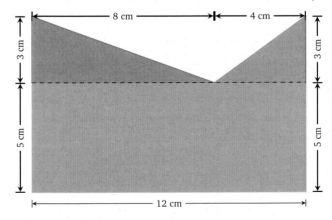

Area of rectangle + Area of left triangle + Area of right triangle
$$= (12 \times 5) + \frac{8 \times 3}{2} + \frac{4 \times 3}{2}$$
$$= 60 + 12 + 6$$
$$= 78 \text{ cm}^2$$

◄

▶ *Solution.* [2] Most contractors would calculate the area beginning with the area of the entire rectangle. When completing a job estimate, some *may* subtract the triangle area as shown below.

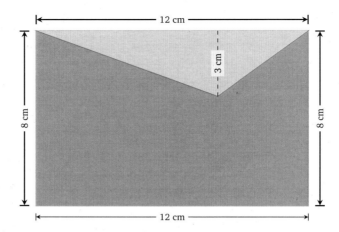

Rectangle Area - Triangle Area

$$= (12 \times 8) - \frac{12 \times 3}{2}$$
$$= 96 - 18$$
$$= 78 \text{ cm}^2$$

◄

The formula for the area of a circle is $A = \pi r^2$, where r is the radius of the circle.

Example 11.3.5. *Determine the area of the following circle with a diameter of 10 cm.*

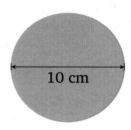

10 cm

▶ *Solution.* $A = \pi r^2$

$$r = \frac{10}{2} = 5$$
$$A = \pi (5)^2$$
$$A = 78.54 \text{ cm} \quad (\text{rounded to two decimal places})$$

◄

Example 11.3.6. *Determine the radius of the circle in **Example 11.3.5** when its area is reduced by 50%.*

▶ **Solution.** Since area calculations use *two* dimensions, the new radius will *not* be 50% of the original radius.

Solve the following equation, accurate to two decimal places.

$$0.50 \left(\pi(5)^2 \right) = \pi r^2$$
$$\frac{0.50 \left(\pi(5)^2 \right)}{\pi} = \frac{\pi r^2}{\pi}$$
$$r^2 = 12.5$$
$$r = \sqrt{12.5}, r > 0$$
$$r \approx 3.54$$

The radius of the circle after its area has been reduced by 50% is 3.54 cm. ◀

11.4 Volume

The interlocking cubes are helpful in developing the concept of volume as they allow us to build three dimensional solids for where we can count the number of cubes that make up the solid. The area formulas developed in two dimensional geometry help us to write volume formulas. Volume is measured in cubic units, such as cm^3, or for liquid measurements, in litres (L). There is a helpful relationship between the two types of volume units: $1 mL = 1 \ cm^3$

We can think of a rectangular prism, basically a shoe box, as its base piled on top of itself many times to make a third dimension, called height. This helps us to visualize the formula for the volume of a prism as V = Area of base × height. The area of the base of the prism can be calculates using the area formulas. In particular, we have the following formulas.

Volume Formulas

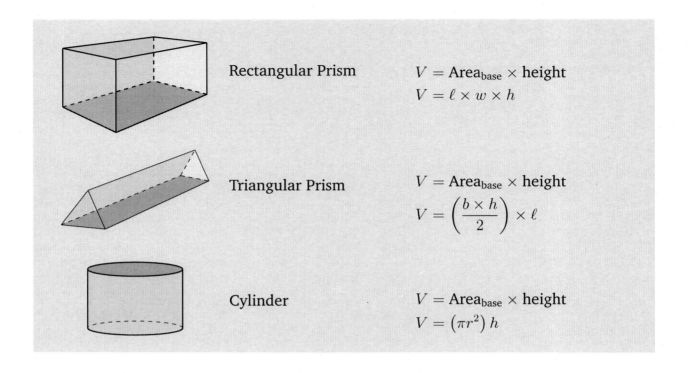

Rectangular Prism	$V = \text{Area}_{\text{base}} \times \text{height}$ $V = \ell \times w \times h$
Triangular Prism	$V = \text{Area}_{\text{base}} \times \text{height}$ $V = \left(\dfrac{b \times h}{2}\right) \times \ell$
Cylinder	$V = \text{Area}_{\text{base}} \times \text{height}$ $V = \left(\pi r^2\right) h$

Example 11.4.1. *Determine the volume of the following rectangular prism.*

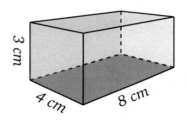

▶ **Solution.** $V = \text{Area}_{\text{base}} \times \text{height}$
$V = \ell \times w \times h$
$V = 8 \times 4 \times 3 = 72\,\text{m}^3$ ◀

Example 11.4.2. *Determine the volume of the following rectangular prism.*

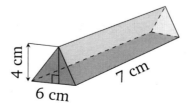

▶ *Solution.* $V = \text{Area}_{\text{base}} \times \text{height}$

$$= \left(\frac{b \times h}{2}\right) \times \ell$$

$$= \left(\frac{6 \times 4}{2}\right) \times 7$$

$$= 84\,\text{cm}^3$$

◀

Example 11.4.3. *Determine the volume of the following cylinder accurate to two decimal places.*

▶ *Solution.* $V = \text{Area}_{\text{base}} \times \text{height}$

$$= \left(\pi r^2\right) h$$

$$= \left(\pi\,(5)^2\right) 12$$

$$\approx 942.48\,\text{mm}^3$$

◀

How does the volume of a pyramid compare with that of a rectangular prism? Suppose we have a container in the shape of a square base pyramid and another container in the shape of a rectangular prism, a shoe box, with same dimensions for base and height. If we filled the pyramid container with water and transferred it to the prism container, we would need to fill the pyramid three times in order to fill the prism. From this experiment it would appear the volume of a pyramid is $\frac{1}{3}$ times the volume of a rectangular prism (and it is). Similarly, the volume of a cone, a 'pointed cylinder', is $\frac{1}{3}$ the volume of a cylinder. This true whenever the new shape is 'pointed'. Recall that in two dimensions the 'pointed' rectangle, a triangle, had an area factor of $\frac{1}{2}$ when compared to the rectangle area. Now in three dimensions, this factor is $\frac{1}{3}$.

Example 11.4.4. *Determine the volume of the following square-based pyramid.*

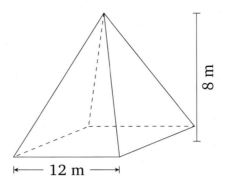

▶ *Solution.*

Volume of pyramid $= \dfrac{1}{3}$ (area of base) $\times$ (height)   ◀

$= \dfrac{1}{3} b^2 \times h$

$= \dfrac{1}{3} (12)^2 \times (8)$

$= 384 \, \text{m}^3$

Example 11.4.5. *Determine the volume of the following cone, accurate to two decimal places.*

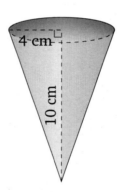

▶ *Solution.*   Volume of cone $= \dfrac{1}{3}$ (area of base) $\times$ (height)   ◀

$= \dfrac{1}{3} \pi r^2 \times h$

$= \dfrac{1}{3} \pi (4)^2 \times (10)$

$\approx 1675.52 \, \text{cm}^3$

$\approx 1.68 \, L$

Example 11.4.6. *Determine the volume of the following sphere accurate to two decimal places.*

← 12 cm →

▶ *Solution.* $r = 6\,\text{cm}$ ◀

$$V = \frac{4}{3}\,r^3 \qquad \textbf{Formula for the volume of a sphere}$$

$$V = \frac{4}{3}\,(6)^3$$

$$V \approx 904.78\,\text{cm}^3$$

11.5   Surface area

SURFACE AREA OF A RECTANGULAR PRISM

The surface area of a solid object is the sum of the area for each face on the object. By 'unfolding' the faces of an object a net can be formed. A net is a two dimensional representation of a 3 dimensional solid. Usually several different nets are possible and help to see the dimensions and shape of each face. The following examples use nets and area formulas to find the surface area of a solid.

Example 11.5.1. *Determine the surface area of the following rectangular prism.*

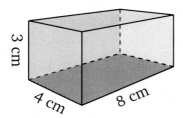

3 cm   4 cm   8 cm

▶ *Solution.* Generate a corresponding net. This net is not unique.

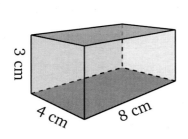

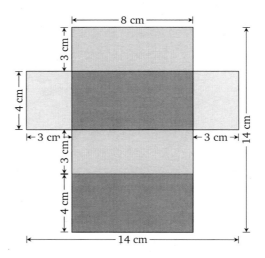

Options:

1. Calculate the area of all faces separately and then add the six areas together.

2. As shown, there are six rectangular faces — three pairs of faces. This illustrates the formula $SA = 2\ell h + 2\ell w + 2hw$.

3. The diagram illustrates a better numeric solution, recognizing one large rectangle and two equal end rectangles.

$$SA = 14 \times 8 + 2\,(3 \times 4) = 136\,\text{cm}^2$$

4. An upper estimate of the surface area is $14 \times 14 = 196\,\text{cm}^2$. The four rectangles that have been included in this estimate can be arranged into one rectangle, and then subtract this area from the upper estimate.

5. Subtract these four areas from the upper estimate.

◀

SURFACE AREA OF A CYLINDER

A cylinder has a net with two circle ends and a rectangle.

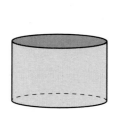
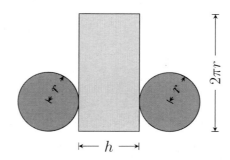

$$SA = 2\pi r^2 + 2\pi rh$$

Example 11.5.2. *Determine the surface area the following cylinder, accurate to two decimal places.*

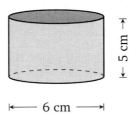

▶ *Solution.*

$$
\begin{aligned}
SA &= 2\pi r^2 + 2\pi r h \\
&= 2\pi(3)^2 + 2\pi(3)(5) \\
&= 56.55 + 94.25 \\
&\approx 150.80 \text{ cm}^2
\end{aligned}
$$

◀

SURFACE AREA OF A SQUARE BASED PYRAMID

A net for a square based pyramid has a square and four congruent triangles.

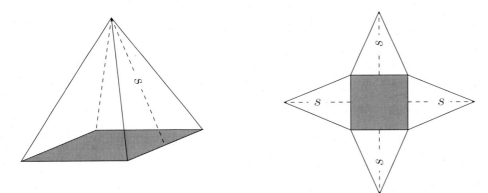

Denoting b as the side length of the square, which is also the base of each triangle and s as the slant height of the pyramid, which is the height of each triangle, we have the surface area of a square based pyramid

$$
\begin{aligned}
SA &= b^2 + 4\left(\frac{1}{2}bh\right) \\
&= b^2 + 2bs
\end{aligned}
$$

Example 11.5.3. *Determine the surface area of the following square based pyramid.*

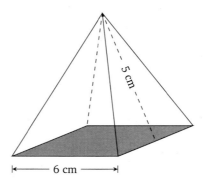

▶ **Solution.** $SA = b^2 + 2bs$

$$= (6)^2 + 2(6)(5)$$
$$= 36 + 60$$
$$= 106 \text{ cm}^2 \qquad \blacktriangleleft$$

SURFACE AREA OF A CONE

The net of a cone consists of a circle with radius r and a sector of another circle with a radius s, where s is the slant height of the cone.

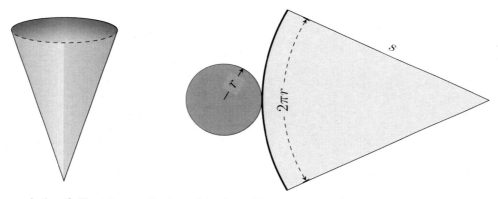

We need the following relationship for the sector and its corresponding circle with radius s.

$$\frac{\text{Area}_{\text{sector}}}{\text{arclength}} = \frac{\text{Area}_{\text{circle}}}{\text{Circumference}}$$

$$\frac{A}{2\pi r} = \frac{\pi s^2}{2\pi s}$$

$$\frac{A}{2\pi r} = \frac{s}{2}$$

$$A = \frac{s}{2}(2\pi r)$$

$$A = \pi r s$$

Th formula for the surface area of a cone is $SA = \pi r^2 + \pi r s$.

Example 11.5.4. *Determine the surface area of the following cone.*

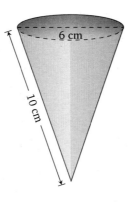

▶ **Solution.** $SA = \pi r^2 + \pi rs$
$$= \pi (6)^2 + \pi (6)(10)$$
$$= 36\pi + 60\pi$$
$$= 96\pi$$
$$\approx 301.59 \text{ cm}^2 \qquad ◀$$

SURFACE AREA OF A SPHERE

The net for a sphere has sections comparable to slicing an orange. The required area calculation is challenging, suggesting an alternate 'net' be used.

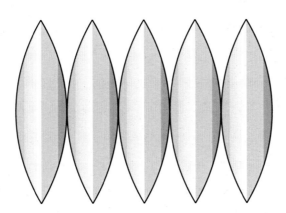

Consider slicing the entire sphere into n square based pyramids, all meeting at the center of the sphere i.e. each height will be the radius of the sphere. The number of pyramids, n, will be controlled by the area, A, of the base of the pyramid.

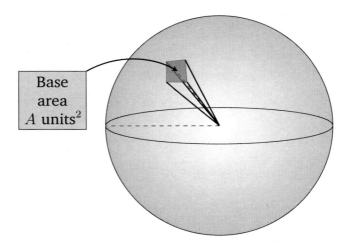

For the sphere, the ratio of surface area to volume will be same as the ratio using the pyramids when the base area of the pyramid is very small and $n \to \infty$. We have the equation

$$\frac{SA_{\text{sphere}}}{V_{\text{sphere}}} = \frac{A_{\text{base of pyramids}}}{V_{\text{pyramids}}}$$

$$= \frac{nA}{n\left(\frac{1}{3}Ar\right)} V_{\text{sphere}}, A \to 0, n \to \infty$$

$$= \frac{1}{\left(\frac{1}{3}r\right)} \left(\frac{4}{3}\pi r^3\right)$$

$$= 4\pi r^2$$

Example 11.5.5. *Determine the surface area of a sphere with a radius of 6 cm, accurate to two decimal places.*

▶ *Solution.* $A = 4\pi r^2$
$$= 4\pi \left(6\right)^2$$
$$\approx 452.39 \text{ cm}^2 \qquad\qquad\qquad\qquad\qquad\qquad\qquad ◀$$

11.6 Pythagorean theorem

The Pythagorean Theorem is named after a Greek Mathematician named Pythagoras, who is credited with discovering a relationship among the sides of a right angled triangle. The area of the square constructed with the hypotenuse as its base has the same area as the sum of the squares constructed on the other two sides. Geometrically, the theorem looks like the following diagram.

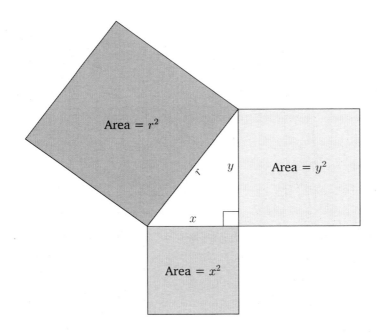

Figure 11.6.1: Illustration of Pythagoras' Theorem

Algebraically, we have $x^2 + y^2 = r^2$, where r is the hypotenuse (the longest side of the triangle, across from the $90°$ angle), and x and y are the legs of the triangle (the connected sides that form the $90°$ angle).

Example 11.6.1. *Determine the length of the hypotenuse in a triangle where the remaining sides have length 3 cm and 4 cm.*

▶ *Solution.* Since there is an hypotenuse, the triangle is right angled.

$$x^2 + y^2 = r^2$$
$$(3)^2 + (4)^2 = r^2$$
$$r^2 = 9 + 16$$
$$r^2 = 25$$
$$r = 5\,\text{cm} \quad \because r > 0$$

Note that this side length is larger than the other two sides, as required since this side is the hypotenuse. ◀

Example 11.6.2. *The straight section of a starting ramp for a 120 m ski jump is to be built with a (vertical) height of 72 m for this section. Determine the required horizontal distance for this portion of the ramp.*

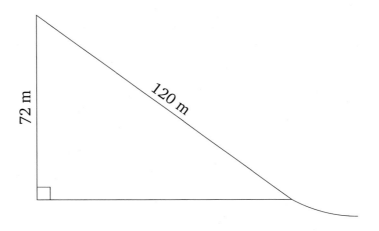

▶ **Solution.**

$$x^2 + y^2 = r^2$$
$$x^2 + (72)^2 = (120)^2$$
$$x^2 = 14\,400 - 5184$$
$$x^2 = 9216$$
$$x = 96\,\text{m}, \quad \because x > 0$$

Note that this side length is smaller than the hypotenuse as required, and is larger than the height. (This is a reasonable expectation for safety – no field trips are planned to test this jump.) ◀

Example 11.6.3. *A shed is to be constructed as shown below. Determine the dimensions of the shed so that the area of the shed is 100 ft².*

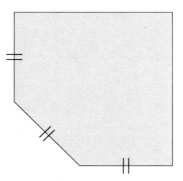

▶ **Solution.** Let x represent the length of the equal side (in ft), and let q represent the length that would complete a 'square' shed (in ft).

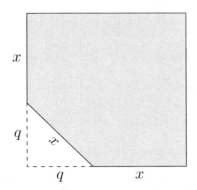

Using Pythagoras' theorem with the triangle, we have

$$q^2 + q^2 = x^2$$
$$2q^2 = r^2$$
$$q^2 = \frac{1}{2}r^2$$
$$q \approx 0.7071r \quad \because q > 0$$

The required area calculation is

$$\text{A}_{\text{square}} - \text{A}_{\text{triangle}} = 100$$
$$(x + q)^2 - \frac{1}{2}q^2 = 100$$
$$(x + 0.7071x)^2 - \frac{1}{2}(0.7071x)^2 = 100$$
$$(1.7071x)^2 - \frac{1}{2}\left(\frac{1}{2}x^2\right) = 100$$
$$2.9142x^2 - 0.25x^2 = 100$$
$$2.6612x^2 = 100$$
$$x^2 = 37.5349$$
$$x \approx 6.13\,\text{ft}$$
$$q \approx (0.7071)\,6.13$$
$$= 4.33\,\text{ft}$$

Each foot has 12 inches, giving a shed plan with the following dimensions.

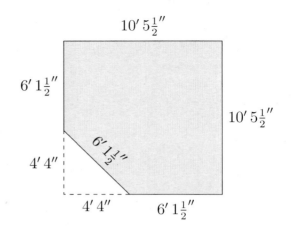

EXERCISES

Exercise 11.1. Consider a convex regular pentagon.

a) Calculate the sum of the interior angles.

b) Calculate the measure of one interior angle.

c) Calculate the measure of one exterior angle.

d) How many lines of symmetry does the regular pentagon have?

e) What are the degrees of rotational symmetry for a regular pentagon?

Exercise 11.2. Complete the following for a hexagonal prism.

a) Sketch a hexagonal prism.

b) Determine the number of faces, edges and vertices

c) Verify that $F + V - 2 = E$

Exercise 11.3. A cylinder has a height of 25 cm and a diameter of 10 cm. Calculate the volume and the surface area.

Exercise 11.4. An open (without a top) rectangular prism has a length of 8 m, a width of 5 m and a height of 4 m. Calculate the volume and surface area.

Exercise 11.5. A square based pyramid has a perpendicular height of 12 cm and a square side length of 10 cm. Use the Pythagorean theorem to calculate the slant height, and then use a net to find the surface area of the pyramid.

Exercise 11.6. A sphere has a radius of 15 cm. Calculate its volume and surface area.

COORDINATE GEOMETRY

INTRODUCTION

When travelling by rail, train or subway, everyone is limited by the track and is forced to follow a line or path. Subways even call their *path* a line. All locations that are not on this line require a transfer to another method of travel. In this section we will introduce a two-dimensional grid, and the corresponding connections between geometry and algebra.

COORDINATE PLANES

There are cities where the road structure is rectangular. For example, Calgary is separated into four geographical quadrants: NE, NW, SE, and SW. For most of the city, the dividing line between North and South is the Bow River with some adjustments for the course of the river. The dividing line between East and West is Centre Street. Streets run north-south. Avenues run east-west.[1] Manhattan has a more obvious grid road structure when using Google Maps.

---

[1]http://calgaryminiguide.blogspot.ca/2009/05/basics-of-calgarys-grid-system.html

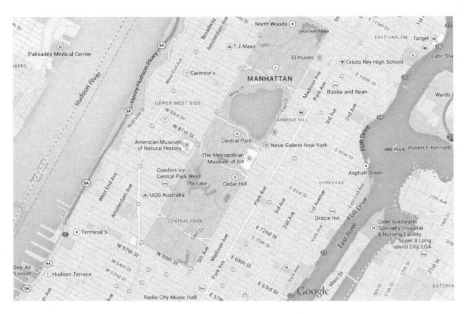

Figure 12.1.1: Manhattan, NY

Geometrically in 2D, two number lines are arranged at a right angle with the x axis as the East-West line, and the y axis as the North-South line. The intersection of the two number lines is called the origin. Every point on this mathematical map has coordinates. The origin has coordinates $(0,0)$. In 3D, the origin coordinates are $(0,0,0)$. All points in 2D have coordinates in the form (left direction, right direction) with direction numbers positive when right or above the origin and negative otherwise. Quadrants are numbered counterclockwise beginning in the NE quadrant.

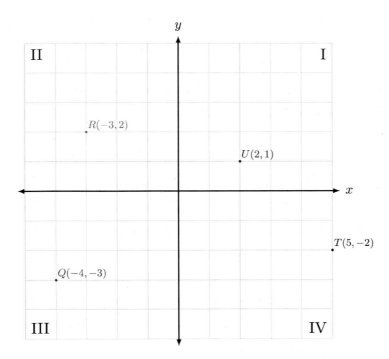

Figure 12.1.2: quadrants and sample points

x	⟲ y
2	1
-3	2
-4	-3
5	-2
2	1

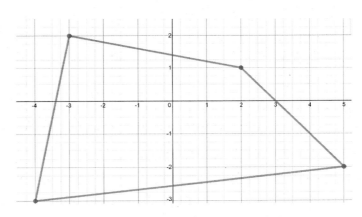

Figure 12.1.3: Add a duplicate first point to close the diagram.

Figure 12.1.4: Joining the points using Desmos software

OPTIONS FOR A NON-MATH CLASS

- One of the assignments given after reading some books is to construct the town *as described in the story*. An initial grid can be constructed using square tiles and used to establish distances. (Possibly the tiles on the floor will already have the grid completed.) The town structure can then be completed using sets of replica buildings etc complete with a transportation system.

- For non-artists who intend to duplicate a section of a drawing by hand, a grid can be superimposed on the original diagram to assist in the dimensions. There is an opportunity here to adjust dimensions by changing the grid structure on the original diagram. For example, height of the original can be decreased using tall rectangles on the original but squares on the final product.

12.2 Slope

Definition 3 (Slope). *For any two points $A(x_1, y_1)$ and $B(x_2, y_2)$, the slope of the line that passes through them is given by the formula*

$$m = \frac{\triangle y}{\triangle x} = \frac{y_2 - y_1}{x_2 - x_1}$$

Example 12.2.1. *Calculate the slope of the line that passes through the points $A(2, 1)$ and $B(7, 4)$.*

▶ *Solution.* SIMPLE SUBSTITUTION - *Minimal thinking required!*
Select $x_1 = 2, y_1 = 1, x_2 = 7, y_2 = 4$ and substitute directly into the stated formula.

$$m = \frac{y_2 - y_1}{x_2 - x_1} = \frac{(4) - (1)}{(7) - (2)} = \frac{3}{5}$$

◀

▶ *Solution.* ORGANIZE, SKETCH, CALCULATE, ANALYZE

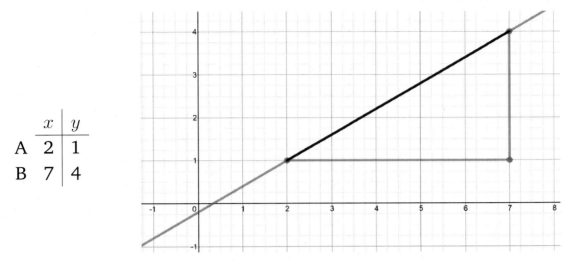

	x	y
A	2	1
B	7	4

Figure 12.2.1: The sketch shows a positive slope, $0 < m < 1$.

The slope can be read direct from this sketch, $m = \frac{\triangle y}{\triangle x} = \frac{3}{5}$.
Also from this sketch: the y intercept is ≈ -0.2, and the x intercept is ≈ 0.3.

	x	y
B	7	4
A	2	1
Subtract	5	3
	$\triangle x$	$\triangle y$

$$m = \frac{3}{5}$$

$$m = \frac{y_2 - y_1}{x_2 - x_1}$$
$$= \frac{(4) - (1)}{(7) - (2)}$$
$$= \frac{3}{5}$$

If the order of the points is reversed, we have no change in the slope.

	x	y
A	2	1
B	7	4
Subtract	-5	-3
	$\triangle x$	$\triangle y$

$$m = \frac{-3}{-5} = \frac{3}{5}$$

$$m = \frac{y_2 - y_1}{x_2 - x_1}$$
$$= \frac{(1) - (4)}{(2) - (7)}$$
$$= \frac{-3}{-5}$$
$$= \frac{3}{5}$$

USING A CALCULATOR

Students who use a calculator may calculate the following slopes.

Correctly   *Incorrectly*

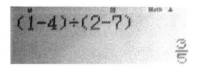   

Since the sketch showed the slope is less than 1, students can recognize an error has been made and edit with pairs of brackets included.

◄

As illustrated below, there are four possible results from slope calculations: positive, negative, zero, and undefined.

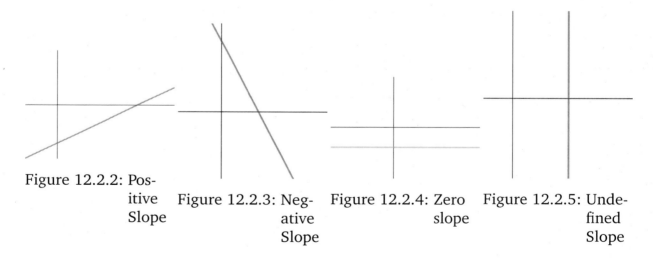

Figure 12.2.2: Pos-itive Slope   Figure 12.2.3: Neg-ative Slope   Figure 12.2.4: Zero slope   Figure 12.2.5: Unde-fined Slope

12.3   The Equation of a Line

In two dimensions, *any* equation with one or two variables *both* with an exponent of 1 and in separate terms, or can be written in separate terms, will be linear and graph as a line.

Example 12.3.1. *(Line Equations)*

- $y = 2x - 3$

- $x = 1$

- $5x - 2y + 10 = 0$

- $\dfrac{y - 4}{x + 1} = \dfrac{3}{5} \rightarrow y - 4 = \dfrac{3}{5}(x + 1)$

Example 12.3.2. *(Equations that are not lines)*

- $y = x^2 - 3$ *does not have exponents of 1 on both variables (a parabola)*

- $xy = 1$ *does not have variables as separate terms and the equivalent form* $y = \dfrac{1}{x} = x^{-1}$ *does not have exponents of 1 (a hyperbola)*

- $y = |2x + 3|$ *includes the variable x in another operation (graphs as a 'V')*

Each of the above equations can be graphed using various software packages.

Definition 4. *[Line] The shortest distance between two points is a line segment. When this segment is extended forever from each end, the corresponding line occurs.*

All line segments selected from this line have the same slope.

From this definition, the equation of a line can be determined through any two points, expecting slope as a required calculation. Sometimes the slope is calculated already and will remove a step from the solution.

Example 12.3.3. *Determine an equation of the line passing through $C(-1, 5)$ and $D(9, 2)$.*

▶ *Solution.*

ORGANIZE AND SKETCH

Selecting the better order of points, we have

	x	y
D	9	2
C	-1	5

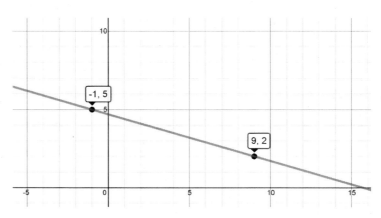

Figure 12.3.1: The sketch shows a negative slope, $-1 < m < 0$, y intercept ≈ 4.5, x intercept ≈ 15.5.

CALCULATE THE SLOPE

	x	y
D	9	2
C	-1	5
Subtract	10	-3
	$\triangle x$	$\triangle y$

$$m = \frac{-3}{10}$$

$$m = \frac{y_2 - y_1}{x_2 - x_1}$$
$$= \frac{(5) - (2)}{(-1) - (9)}$$
$$= \frac{3}{-10}$$

SELECT A GENERAL POINT ON THE LINE $P(x, y)$ AND CALCULATE THE SLOPE

	x	y
P		
D	9	2
Subtract	$x - 9$	$y - 2$
	$\triangle x$	$\triangle y$

$$m = \frac{y - 2}{x - 9}$$

$$m = \frac{y_2 - y_1}{x_2 - x_1}$$
$$= \frac{y - 2}{x - 9}$$

WRITE THE LINE EQUATION

Using definition 4, the line equation is

$$\frac{y-2}{x-9} = \frac{-3}{10}$$

After multiplying both sides by $x - 9$ this equation can be rewritten

$$y - 2 = -\frac{3}{10}(x - 9)$$

◄

ALTERNATE FORMS

There are several forms that may be requested for final answers, but the forms are all linear.

form name	equation	applications
Slope (definition)	$\frac{y-y_0}{x-x_0} = m$	Always works
Slope - point	$y - y_0 = m(x - x_0)$	a faster version of the definition*
Slope - y intercept	$y = mx + b$	easiest for determing additional points*
Vertical line	$x = a$	*an *exception* generated by previous forms
Linear System	$ax + by = c$	solving a system of equations by elimination
Standard	$ax + by + c = 0$	distance calculations, conics

ALTERNATE FORM TO COMPLETE THE FINAL STEPS OF EXAMPLE 12.3.3

With the slope calculated to be $\frac{-3}{10}$, use the form $y = \frac{-3}{10}x + b$ and one of the points. (*Exercise*: Show either point can be used and the final equation wil be the same.)

Selecting the *easier* point $D(9, 2)$ to calculate with, the coordinates can be substituted into the line equation.

$$y = \frac{-3}{10}x + b$$
$$(2) = \frac{-3}{10}(9) + b$$
$$20 = -27 + 10b$$
$$10b = 47$$
$$b = \frac{47}{10}$$

The final equation is $y = -\frac{3}{10}x + \frac{47}{10}$.

NOTES

- This solution is often recommended but always generates more mechanical errors than any other form.

- The placement of negative signs is required in front of the fraction line on all final answers.

- Excellent equation solving skills are required.

- Integer coordinates may be challenging to find for this example.

- This format increases arithmetic challenges if the x intercept was required.

- Consider using the following theorem instead

CALCULATING SLOPE WITHOUT THE SLOPE FORMULA

Using only the model $y = mx + b$ and two points, the slope can be determined *without* the slope formula.

Using example 12.3.3

$$
\begin{array}{cc|c}
 & x & y \\
\hline
D & 9 & 2 \\
C & -1 & 5 \\
\end{array}
$$

$\begin{aligned} &\rightarrow & 2 &= 9m + b \\ &\rightarrow & 5 &= -m + b \end{aligned}$

$$\text{Subtract} \quad -3 = 10m$$

$$m = -\frac{3}{10}$$

Theorem 1. *(Slope Point Equation of a Line) The equation of a line passing through the point $P(x_0, y_0)$ with slope $m, m \neq 0$ can be determined by the equation*

$$y - y_0 = m(x - x_0)$$

Example 12.3.4. *Determine the equation of a line passing through $E(1, -2)$ with a slope of $\frac{2}{3}$.*

▶ *Solution.*

SKETCH

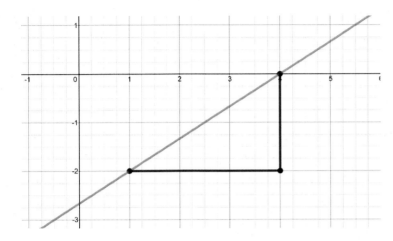

The sketch shows the y intercept ≈ -2.6, and the x intercept 4.

SLOPE - POINT EQUATION OF A LINE

Since the slope was given, no slope calculations are required.

This line is not vertical, select the model $y - y_0 = m \left(x - x_0 \right)$, a variation of the line definition.

Substituting the variables into the formula we have

$$y - y_0 = m \left(x - x_0 \right)$$
$$y - (-2) = \frac{2}{3} \left(x - 1 \right)$$
$$y + 2 = \frac{2}{3} \left(x - 1 \right)$$

If slope - y intercept form was required, we have

$$y + 2 = \frac{2}{3}x - \frac{2}{3}$$
$$y = \frac{2}{3}x - \frac{8}{3}$$

The y intercept of $-\frac{8}{3} \approx -2.67$ is consistent with the estimate from the sketch. ◄

12.4   Parallel and Perpendicular Lines

As stated in definition 4, all line segments selected from a line have the same slope. Any other line segments or lines with the same slope are parallel to this line.

Definition 5 (Perpendicular Lines). *Two lines are perpendicular when the measure of the angle between the lines is* 90°.

Numerically
For lines not parallel to the axes, the slopes of perpendicular lines are related by the formula $m_1 m_2 = -1$. *Each slope is the negative reciprocal of the other.*

A line with a slope of zero is perpendicular to a line with an undefined slope.

Example 12.4.1. *Given the line* $4x + 3y = 12$, *determine the equation of the line passing through* $H(1, -2)$ *that is*

    (a) *parallel to the given line*

    (b) *perpendicular to the given line*

The final form of the line equation is to be in the form $ax + by = c$.

▶ *Solution.*

ORGANIZE AND SKETCH

$$4x + 3y = 12$$

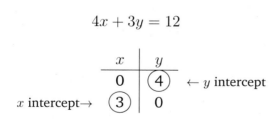

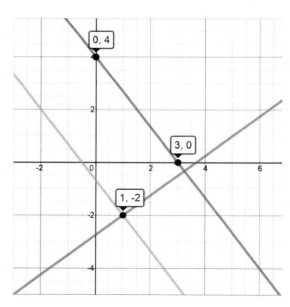

SLOPE OBSERVATIONS

It is *not* necessary to determine the slope of the given line to determine either of the new line equations.

The sketch does show the slope is negative. It can be calculated using any two points on the line, or from the equation when written in the form $y = mx + b$. The current slope is $-\frac{4}{3}$ and the perpendicular slope will be $\frac{3}{4}$.

WRITE THE LINE EQUATION

PARALLEL

Use the parallel model $4x + 3y = c$, and substitute the point coordinates from $H(1, -2)$.

$$4x + 3y = c$$
$$4(1) + 3(-2) = c$$
$$c = -2$$

The equation of the parallel line is $4x + 3y = -2$.

◄

PERPENDICULAR

Use the perpendicular model $3x - 4y = c$, and substitute the point coordinates from $H(1, -2)$. (You can check that the slope of this line is $\frac{3}{4}$.)

$$3x - 4y = c$$
$$3(1) - 4(-2) = c$$
$$c = 11$$

The equation of the perpendicular line is $3x - 4y = 11$.

12.5 Distance formula

Other major cities include at least one ring road. London has constructed several.

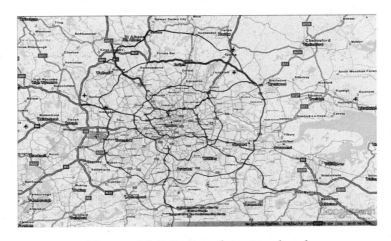

Figure 12.5.1: London, England
`http://1.bp.blogspot.com/-s1J7xu8rpKU/`
`U43mSHcDxgI/AAAAAAAAAgY/A78OPG2ewCA/s1600/`
`Ringways+and+radials+complete+London.jpg`

Each 'circular' road has a radius where the distance from a centre point is constant. Pythagoras' theorem applied to a circle drawn on a grid with centre $(0, 0)$ has the equation $x^2 + y^2 = r^2$.

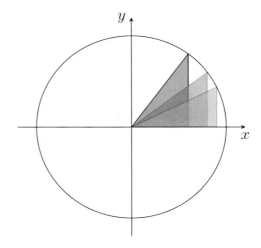

Figure 12.5.2: the circle $x^2 + y^2 = r^2$

If the centre is any point (h, k), the circle equation becomes

$$r^2 = (\triangle x)^2 + (\triangle y)^2$$
$$r^2 = (x - h)^2 + (y - k)^2$$

The distance between any two points can be calculated using the same formula, however it is often written

$$r^2 = (\triangle x)^2 + (\triangle y)^2$$
$$\text{distance} = \sqrt{(\triangle x)^2 + (\triangle y)^2}$$
$$\text{distance} = \sqrt{(x_2 - x_1)^2 + (y_2 - y_1)^2}$$

The $\triangle x$ and $\triangle y$ variables are the same that were calculated when the slope of a line was required in chapter 12.2.

Example 12.5.1. *Determine the distance between $(2, 1)$ and $(7, 4)$.*

▶ *Solution.*

x	y
7	4
2	1

Subtract	5	3
	$\triangle x$	$\triangle y$

$$\text{distance} = \sqrt{(\triangle x)^2 + (\triangle y)^2}$$
$$= \sqrt{(5)^2 + (3)^2}$$
$$= \sqrt{25 + 9}$$
$$= \sqrt{34}$$
$$\approx 5.83 \text{ units}$$

Using the formula directly we have

$$\text{distance} = \sqrt{(x_2 - x_1)^2 + (y_2 - y_1)^2}$$
$$= \sqrt{((7) - (2))^2 + ((4) - (1))^2}$$
$$= \sqrt{(5)^2 + (3)^2}$$
$$= \sqrt{25 + 9}$$
$$= \sqrt{34}$$
$$\approx 5.83 \text{ units}$$

◀

Example 12.5.2. *Determine the equation of the circle with centre* $(0,0)$ *and passing through the point* $(4, -3)$.

▶ *Solution.* Since the centre is $(0,0)$, the equation $x^2 + y^2 = r^2$ is the 'model' equation to use. After substituting the coordinates of the point $(4, -3)$, the radius can be calculated (if required).

$$x^2 + y^2 = r^2$$
$$(4)^2 + (-3)^2 = r^2$$
$$16 + 9 = r^2$$
$$r^2 = 25$$

The equation of the circle is $x^2 + y^2 = 25$ ◀

12.6 Midpoint

When two people are negotiating the price for some item, usually one negotiator suggests a lower price than the other. A simple decision for the next step is to 'meet' the other half-way. This is the average, the midpoint, of the two prices. For two points in two dimensions, the easiest method of determining the midpoint $M(x, y)$ between two points $A(x_1, y_1)$, and $B(x_2, y_2)$ is

$$x = \frac{x_1 + x_2}{2}$$
$$y = \frac{y_1 + y_2}{2}$$

Example 12.6.1. *Determine the coordinates of the midpoint of the line segment joining* $A(5, 6)$ *and* $A(-3, 0)$

▶ **Solution.** Using the formula, we have

$$x = \frac{(5) + (-3)}{2}$$
$$= -1$$
$$y = \frac{(6) + (0)}{2}$$
$$= 3$$

The midpoint of the line segment AB is $(-1, 3)$.

A distance check can be made from this point to A and then to B, but this calculation alone will *not* guarantee the midpoint is correct. There are an infinite number of points that are an equal distance from A and B.

For any point that lies on the perpendicular bisector of the line segment joining A and B, the distance to the two points A and B will be equal.

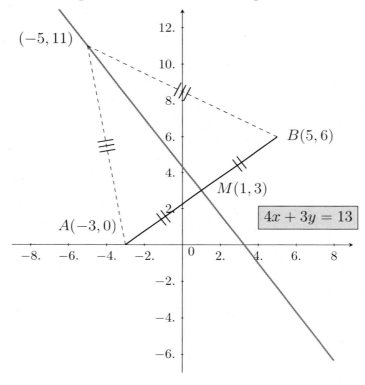

12.7   Reflections, Rotations and Translations

Every day, at some point in the day, everyone 'looks in the mirror' (and makes minor 'repairs'), travels somewhere, and most likely makes at least one turn on the way. You have completed three mathematical operations: reflect, translate, and rotate.

TRANSLATIONS

When an object has been translated, each part of the object moves the same distance, in the same direction. Basically a 'one-yard rush' play in football where *all* players attempt to move forward one yard (and one player is holding the ball).

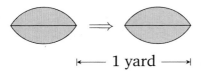

$$\longleftarrow 1 \text{ yard} \longrightarrow$$

Figure 12.7.1: The one yard play $(x, y) \to (x + 1, y)$

In two dimensions, a translation of h units horizontally, and k units vertically is written.

$$(x, y) \to (x + h, y + k)$$

ROTATIONS

When an object is rotated, each part of the object rotates around one point. In ballet, a pirouette is a (successful) spin when balanced on the toe of (usually) one shoe.

The centre of any rotation can be determined by constructing a perpendicular bisector for each line segment between corresponding points. All the bisectors will meet at the centre of rotation.

Example 12.7.1. *Determine the centre of rotation for the following object captured using 'time lapse photography'.*

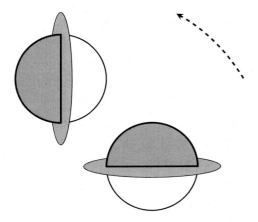

▶ *Solution.* Additional key points Q and Q' were introduced at the midpoint of the shaded semicircle on both photos. Without them all perpendicular bisectors of line segments between corresponding key points will be the same.

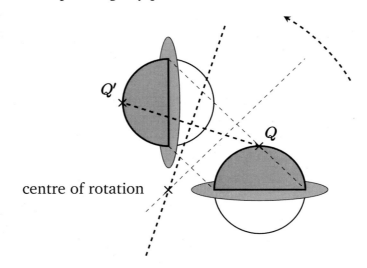

Figure 12.7.2: Rotation of $90°$ $(x, y) \rightarrow (-y, x)$

◀

REFLECTIONS

Every reflection in a line preserves every length and angle but reverses any order of labelling.

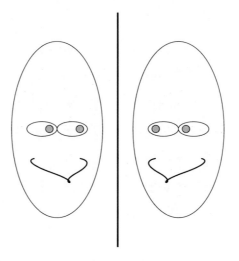

Figure 12.7.3: Mirror Reflection $(x, y) \rightarrow (-x, y)$

EXERCISES

Exercise 12.1. Answer the following.

a) Determine the slope and the equation of the line connecting $(-4, -3)$ and $(5, 9)$. Graph the line.

b) Calculate the distance from $(-2, -5)$ to $(2, 1)$.

c) Determine the equation of a line parallel to $y = 3x5$ and passing through $(-1, -7)$

d) Determine the equation of a line perpendicular to $y = 2x + 1$ and passing through $(-4, 5)$

e) Determine the x and y intercepts of $3x - 2y = 9$, and then use the intercepts to graph the line.

INDEX